Contents

Meat and Poultry 2

Casseroles 16

Soups and Salads 30

Side Dishes 44

Cakes and Pies 56

Desserts 66

Cookies and Brownies 78

Acknowledgments 94

Index 95

Meat and Poultry

Herbed Chicken & Vegetables

2 medium all-purpose potatoes, thinly sliced (about 1 pound)
2 medium carrots, sliced
4 bone-in chicken pieces (about 2 pounds)
1 envelope LIPTON® RECIPE SECRETS® Savory Herb with Garlic Soup Mix
1/3 cup water
1 tablespoon BERTOLLI® Olive Oil

1. Preheat oven to 425°F. In broiler pan without the rack, place potatoes and carrots; arrange chicken on top. Pour soup mix blended with water and oil over chicken and vegetables.

2. Bake uncovered 40 minutes or until chicken is thoroughly cooked, juices run clear and vegetables are tender.   Makes 4 servings

Prep Time: 10 minutes
Cook Time: 40 minutes

Herbed Chicken & Vegetables

Meat and Poultry

Buttermilk Oven-Fried Chicken

1½ cups buttermilk
4 teaspoons garlic powder, divided
2 teaspoons salt
2 teaspoons dried thyme, divided
1 teaspoon dried sage
1 teaspoon paprika
½ teaspoon black pepper
2½ pounds chicken pieces, skin removed
Nonstick cooking spray
1½ cups dry bread crumbs
¼ cup all-purpose flour

1. Whisk buttermilk, 3 teaspoons garlic powder, salt, 1 teaspoon thyme, sage, paprika and pepper in large bowl until well blended. Add chicken; turn to coat. Cover and refrigerate at least 5 hours or overnight.

2. Preheat oven to 400°F. Line 2 baking sheets with foil; spray with cooking spray.

3. Combine bread crumbs, flour, remaining 1 teaspoon garlic powder and 1 teaspoon thyme in large shallow bowl. Remove chicken from buttermilk mixture, allowing excess to drip off. Coat chicken pieces one at a time with crumb mixture. Shake off excess crumbs. Place on prepared baking sheets; let stand 10 minutes.

4. Spray top portions of chicken with cooking spray. Bake about 50 minutes or until chicken is golden brown and juices run clear, turning once and spraying with additional cooking spray halfway through baking time.

Makes about 8 servings

Buttermilk Oven-Fried Chicken

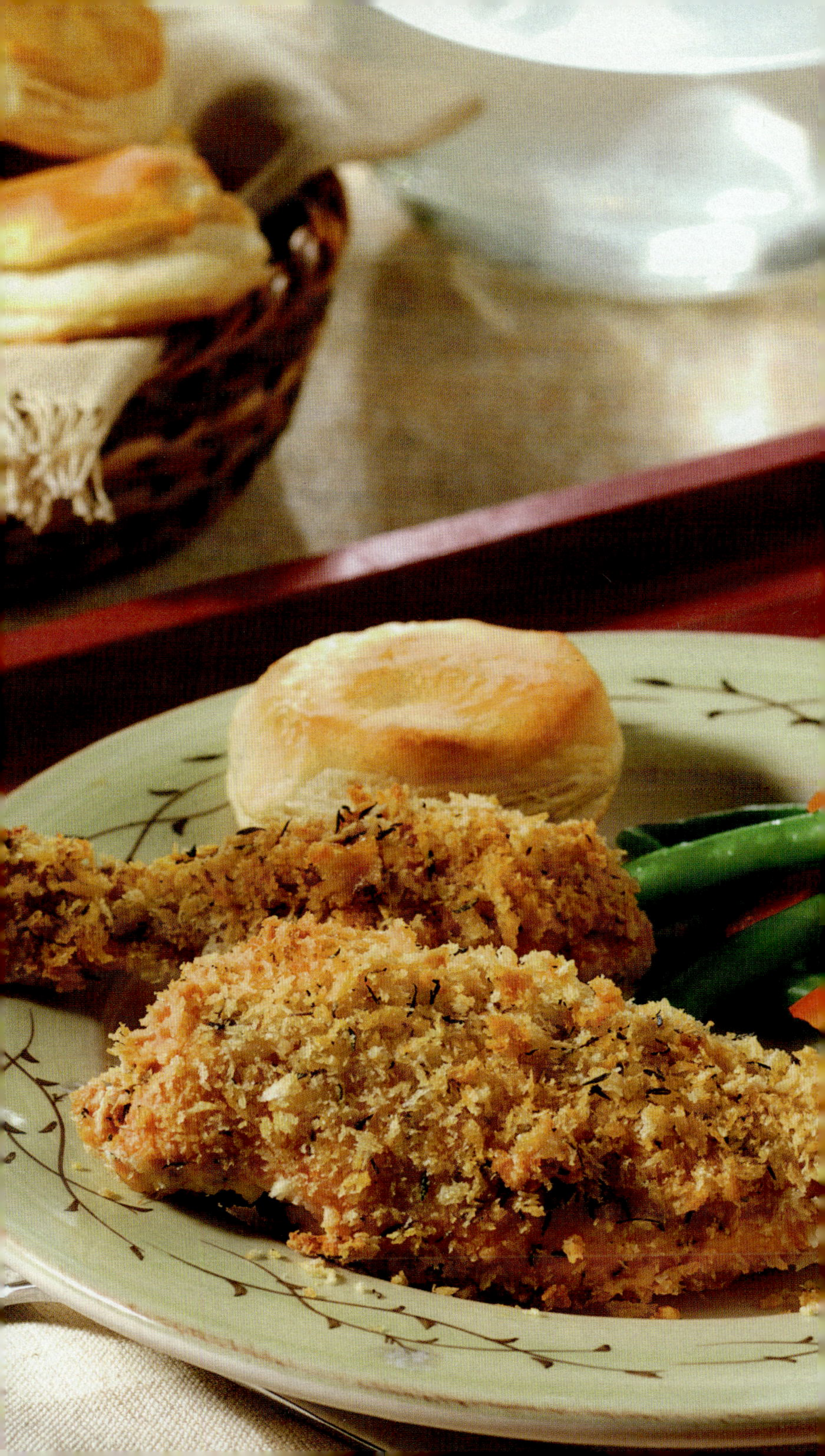

Meat and Poultry

Maple-Mustard Pork Chops

    2 tablespoons maple syrup
    1 tablespoon olive oil
    2 teaspoons whole-grain mustard
    2 center-cut pork loin chops (6 ounces each)
       Nonstick cooking spray
$1/3$ cup water

1. Preheat oven to 375°F. Combine syrup, oil and mustard in small bowl. Brush syrup mixture over both sides of pork chops.

2. Spray medium ovenproof skillet with cooking spray; heat over medium-high heat. Add chops; brown on both sides. Add water; cover and bake 20 to 30 minutes or until barely pink in center.

Makes 2 servings

Kielbasa & Sauerkraut Skillet Dinner

    2 tablespoons olive oil
    1 pound kielbasa sausage, cut into $1/4$-inch slices
    1 small red onion, thinly sliced
    1 small green bell pepper, thinly sliced
    2 cups sauerkraut, rinsed and well drained
    2 teaspoons Dijon mustard
$1/2$ teaspoon caraway seeds
$1/4$ teaspoon salt
$1/4$ teaspoon black pepper

1. Heat oil in large skillet. Add kielbasa, onion and bell pepper. Cook over medium heat 5 to 10 minutes or until vegetables are tender and sausage is lightly browned, stirring occasionally. Drain fat.

2. Add sauerkraut, mustard, caraway seeds, salt and black pepper to skillet. Cook over medium heat 3 to 5 minutes or until heated through.

Makes 4 servings

Maple-Mustard Pork Chop

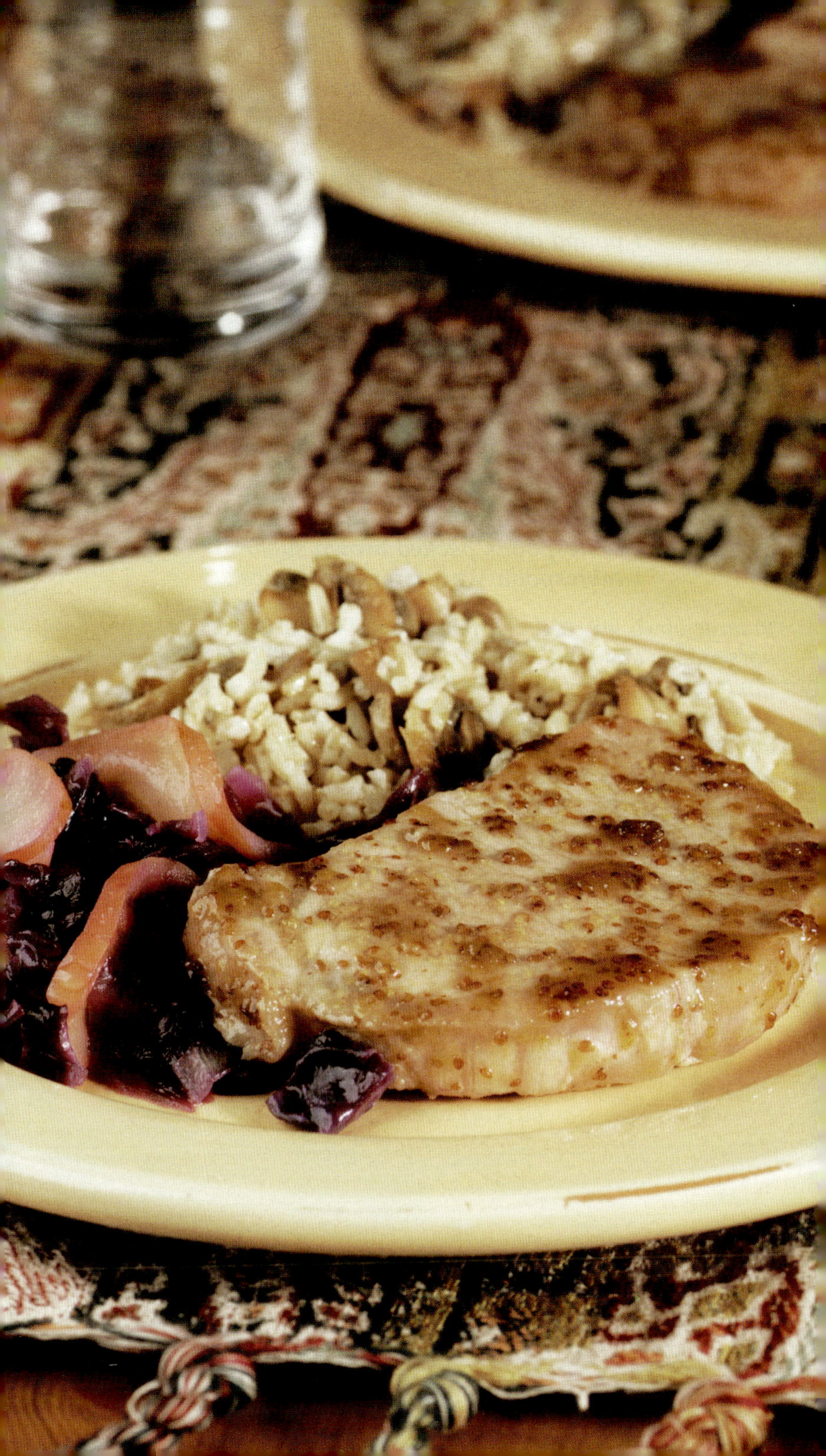

Meat and Poultry

Ham Loaf

1 pound ground pork
1/2 pound ham, ground
3/4 cup milk
1/2 cup fresh bread crumbs
1 egg
1 tablespoon instant tapioca
1/2 teaspoon prepared horseradish
3 to 4 drops red food color (optional)

Sauce
1/2 cup ketchup
2 tablespoons packed brown sugar
1 tablespoon Worcestershire sauce

In large bowl, mix together pork, ham, milk, crumbs, egg, tapioca, horseradish and food color, if desired, until well blended. Place mixture in loaf pan and bake at 325°F for 1 hour. In small bowl, stir together Sauce ingredients. Pour Sauce over Ham Loaf and bake for another 30 minutes, basting occasionally with Sauce. Remove from oven; let stand 10 minutes before removing from pan. Slice to serve.

Makes 6 servings

Prep Time: 10 minutes
Cook Time: 90 minutes

Favorite recipe from **National Pork Board**

Tip: To make fresh bread crumbs, first remove the crusts from two slices of bread, then tear bread into small pieces. Day-old firm-textured bread works best.

Meat and Poultry

Cheesy Ham and Macaroni

1 (1.8 ounce) package white sauce mix
2 cups milk
½ cup grated Parmesan cheese
½ cup cubed American cheese
⅛ teaspoon ground black pepper
7 ounces macaroni, cooked according to package directions, drained
1½ cups diced fully cooked ham
1 cup frozen green peas, thawed

In a large saucepan, stir together white sauce mix and milk.* Following package directions, cook until thickened. Stir in cheeses and pepper. Add macaroni, ham and peas; cook, stirring until heated through. Serve hot. Makes 6 servings

*If you want to make a white sauce from scratch, melt 3 tablespoons butter in a saucepan. Stir in ¼ cup flour and cook until mixture bubbles. Stir in 2 cups milk and cook, stirring, until thickened.

Favorite recipe from **National Pork Board**

Meat and Poultry

Country Chicken Stew with Dumplings

>   1 tablespoon BERTOLLI® Olive Oil
>   1 chicken (3 to 3½ pounds), cut into serving pieces (with or without skin)
>   4 large carrots, cut into 2-inch pieces
>   3 ribs celery, cut into 1-inch pieces
>   1 large onion, cut into 1-inch wedges
>   1 envelope LIPTON® RECIPE SECRETS® Savory Herb with Garlic Soup Mix*
> 1½ cups water
>   ½ cup apple juice
>   Parsley Dumplings (optional, recipe follows)

*Also terrific with LIPTON® RECIPE SECRETS® Golden Onion Soup Mix.

In 6-quart Dutch oven or heavy saucepot, heat oil over medium-high heat and brown ½ of the chicken; remove and set aside. Repeat with remaining chicken. Return chicken to Dutch oven. Stir in carrots, celery, onion, and Savory Herb with Garlic Soup Mix blended with water and apple juice. Bring to a boil over high heat. Reduce heat to low; simmer covered 25 minutes or until chicken is thoroughly cooked, juices run clear and vegetables are tender.

Meanwhile, prepare Parsley Dumplings. Drop 12 rounded tablespoonfuls of batter into simmering broth around chicken. Continue simmering, covered, 10 minutes or until toothpick inserted in center of dumplings comes out clean. Season stew, if desired, with salt and pepper.   *Makes about 6 servings*

Parsley Dumplings: *In medium bowl, combine 1⅓ cups all-purpose flour, 1 tablespoon chopped fresh parsley, 2 teaspoons baking powder and ½ teaspoon salt; set aside. In measuring cup, blend ⅔ cup milk, 1 egg and 2 tablespoons melted butter or margarine. Stir milk mixture into flour mixture just until blended.*

Country Chicken Stew with Dumplings

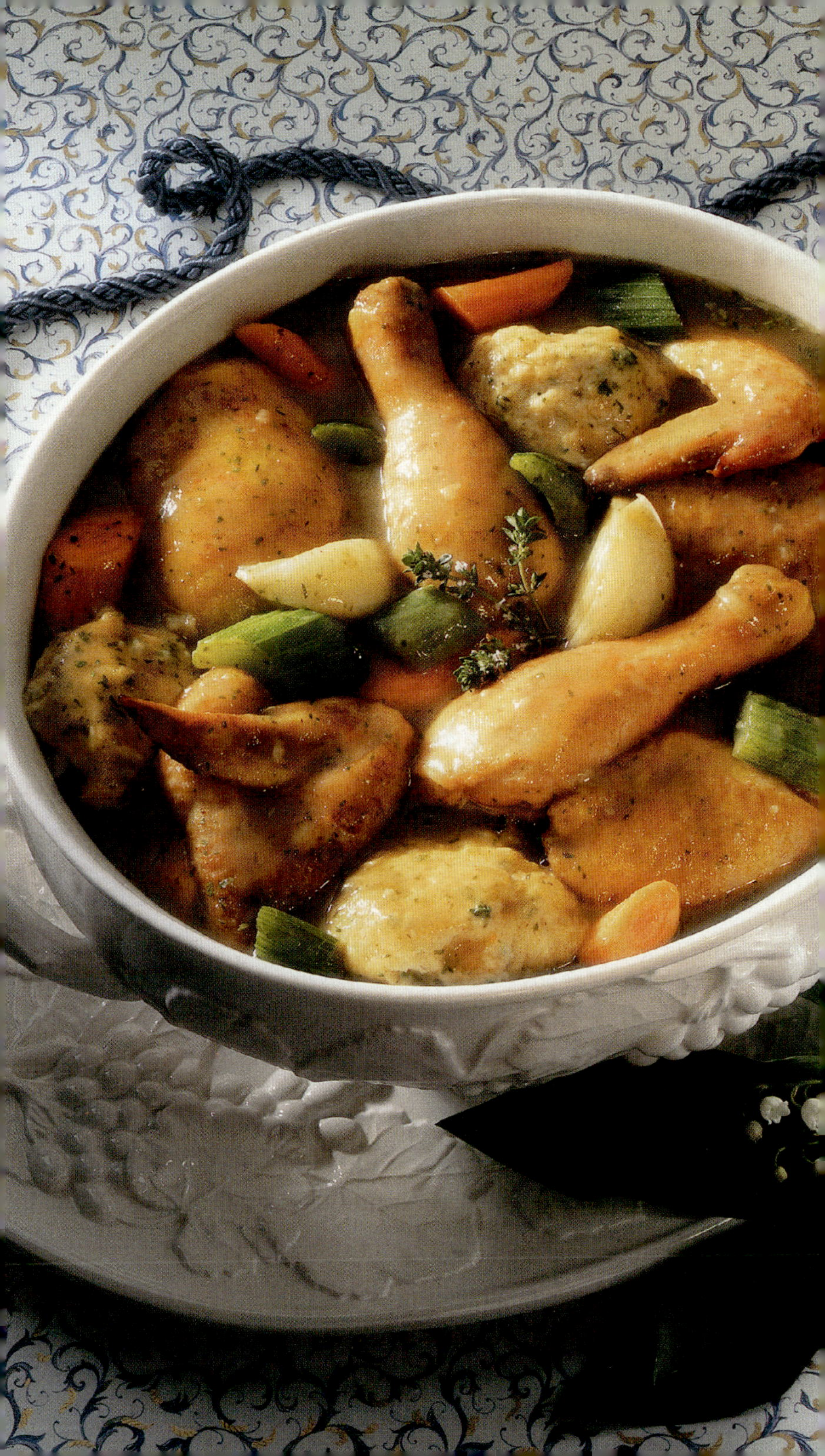

Meat and Poultry

Family-Style Creamy Chicken and Noodles

   8 ounces uncooked yolk-free wide egg noodles
   4 cups water
   1 pound boneless skinless chicken breasts
1½ cups chopped onions
  ¾ cup chopped celery
  ½ teaspoon salt
  ½ teaspoon dried thyme
   1 bay leaf
  ⅛ teaspoon white pepper
   1 can (10¾-ounce) condensed reduced-sodium cream of chicken soup, undiluted
  ½ cup fat-free buttermilk

1. Cook pasta according to package directions, omitting salt. Drain; set aside.

2. Meanwhile, bring water to a boil in Dutch oven over high heat. Add chicken breasts, onions, celery, salt, thyme, bay leaf and pepper. Return to a boil. Reduce heat to low; simmer, uncovered, 35 minutes or until chicken is cooked through. Remove chicken. Cut into ½-inch pieces; set aside.

3. Increase heat to high. Return liquid in Dutch oven to a boil. Continue cooking until liquid and vegetables have reduced to 1 cup. Remove from heat; discard bay leaf. Whisk in soup and buttermilk until well blended. Cook over medium heat until hot. Add chicken pieces and pasta; toss to blend. Sprinkle with parsley, if desired.

Makes 4 servings

Family-Style Creamy Chicken and Noodles

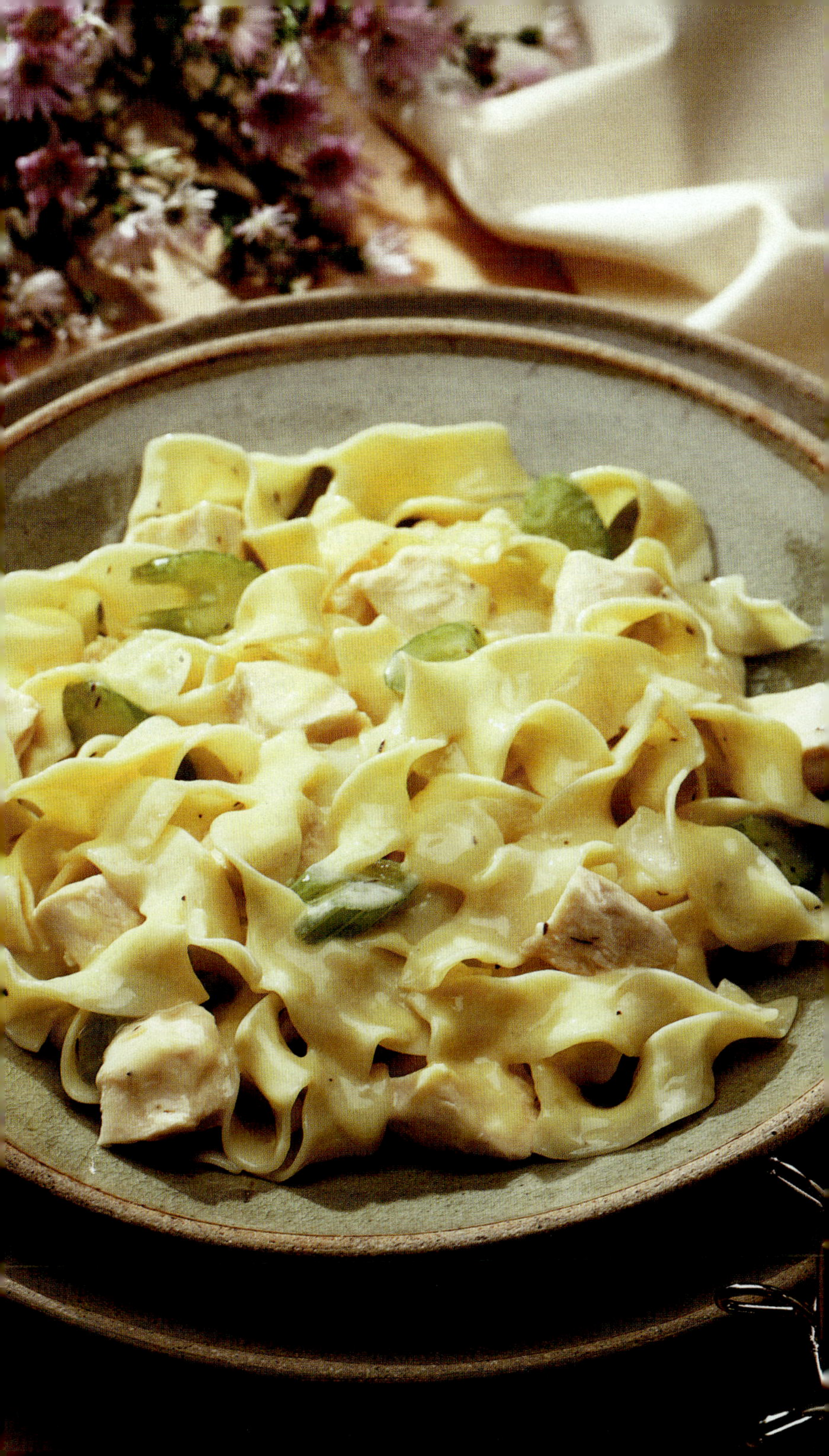

Meat and Poultry

Homestyle Skillet Chicken

1 tablespoon Cajun seasoning blend
1/2 teaspoon plus 1/8 teaspoon black pepper, divided
1/2 teaspoon salt, divided
4 chicken thighs
2 tablespoons vegetable oil
4 cloves garlic, minced
3/4 pound small red or new potatoes (about 8), quartered
12 pearl onions, peeled*
1 cup baby carrots
2 ribs celery, halved lengthwise and sliced diagonally into 1/2-inch pieces
1/2 red bell pepper, diced
2 tablespoons all-purpose flour
1 1/2 cups canned reduced-sodium chicken broth
2 tablespoons finely chopped fresh parsley

To peel pearl onions, drop in boiling water for 30 seconds and plunge immediately into ice water. The peel should slide right off.

1. Combine Cajun seasoning, 1/2 teaspoon pepper and 1/4 teaspoon salt in small bowl. Rub mixture onto all sides of chicken.

2. Heat oil in large heavy skillet over medium-high heat. Add garlic and chicken; cook about 3 minutes per side until chicken is browned. Transfer chicken to plate; set aside.

3. Add potatoes, onions, carrots, celery and bell pepper to skillet. Cook and stir 3 minutes. Sprinkle flour over vegetables; stir to coat. Slowly stir in chicken broth, scraping up browned bits from bottom of skillet. Bring mixture to a boil, stirring constantly.

4. Reduce heat to medium-low. Return chicken to skillet. Cover and cook about 30 minutes or until juices of chicken run clear. Increase heat to medium-high; cook, uncovered, about 5 minutes or until sauce is thickened. Season with remaining 1/4 teaspoon salt and 1/8 teaspoon pepper. Sprinkle with parsley before serving.

Makes 4 servings

Homestyle Skillet Chicken

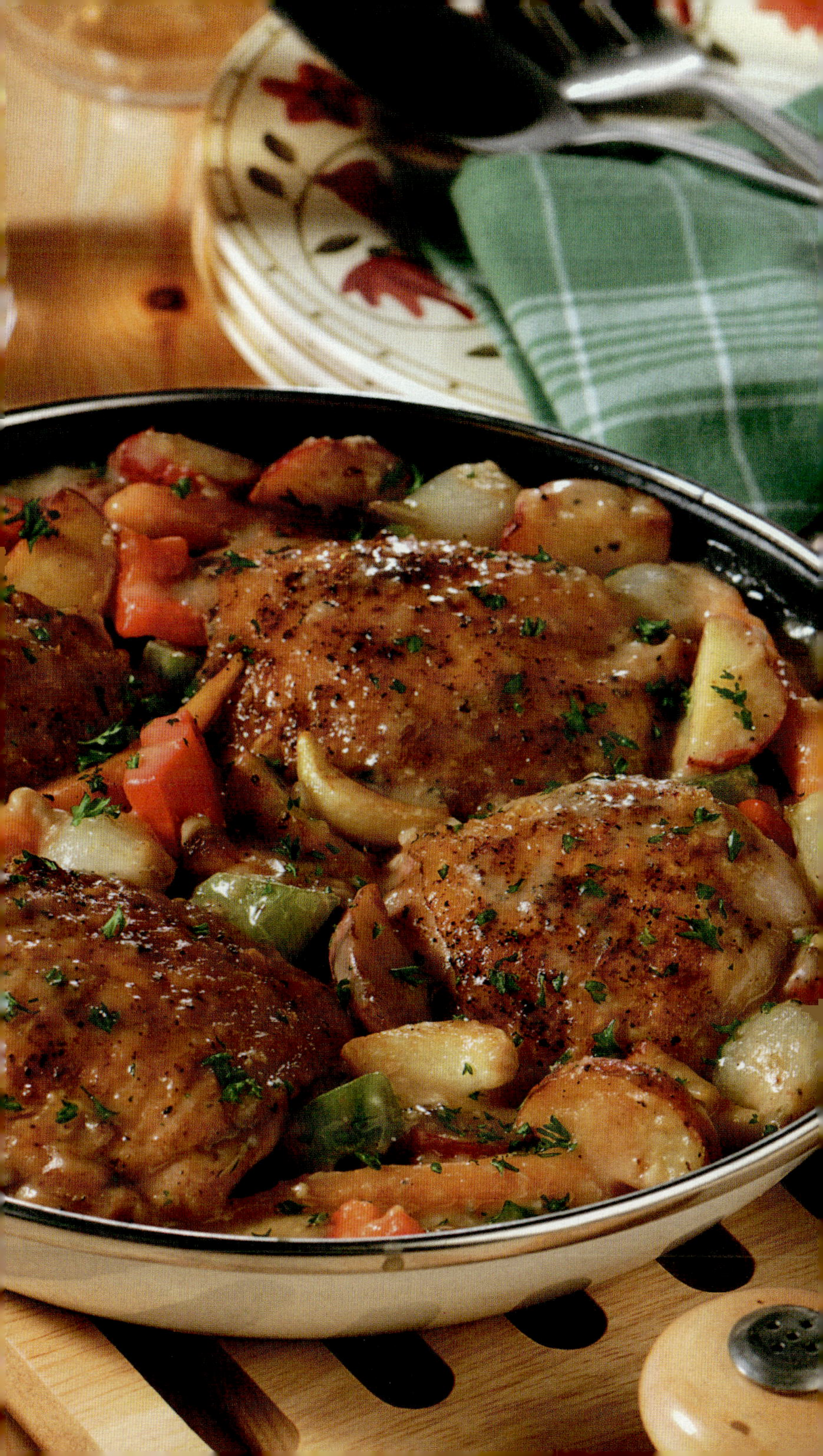

Casseroles

Pork with Savory Apple Stuffing

1 package (6 ounces) corn bread stuffing mix
1 can (14½ ounces) chicken broth
1 small apple, peeled, cored and chopped
¼ cup chopped celery
1⅓ cups French's® French Fried Onions, divided
4 boneless pork chops, ¾ inch thick
  (about 1 pound)
½ cup peach-apricot sweet and sour sauce
1 tablespoon French's® Honey Dijon Mustard

1. Preheat oven to 375°F. Combine stuffing mix, broth, apple, celery and ⅔ cup French Fried Onions in large bowl. Spoon into bottom of greased shallow 2-quart baking dish. Arrange chops on top of stuffing.

2. Combine sweet and sour sauce with mustard in small bowl. Pour over pork. Bake 40 minutes or until pork is no longer pink in center.

3. Sprinkle with remaining onions. Bake 5 minutes or until onions are golden.   Makes 4 servings

Prep Time: 10 minutes
Cook Time: 45 minutes

Pork with Savory Apple Stuffing

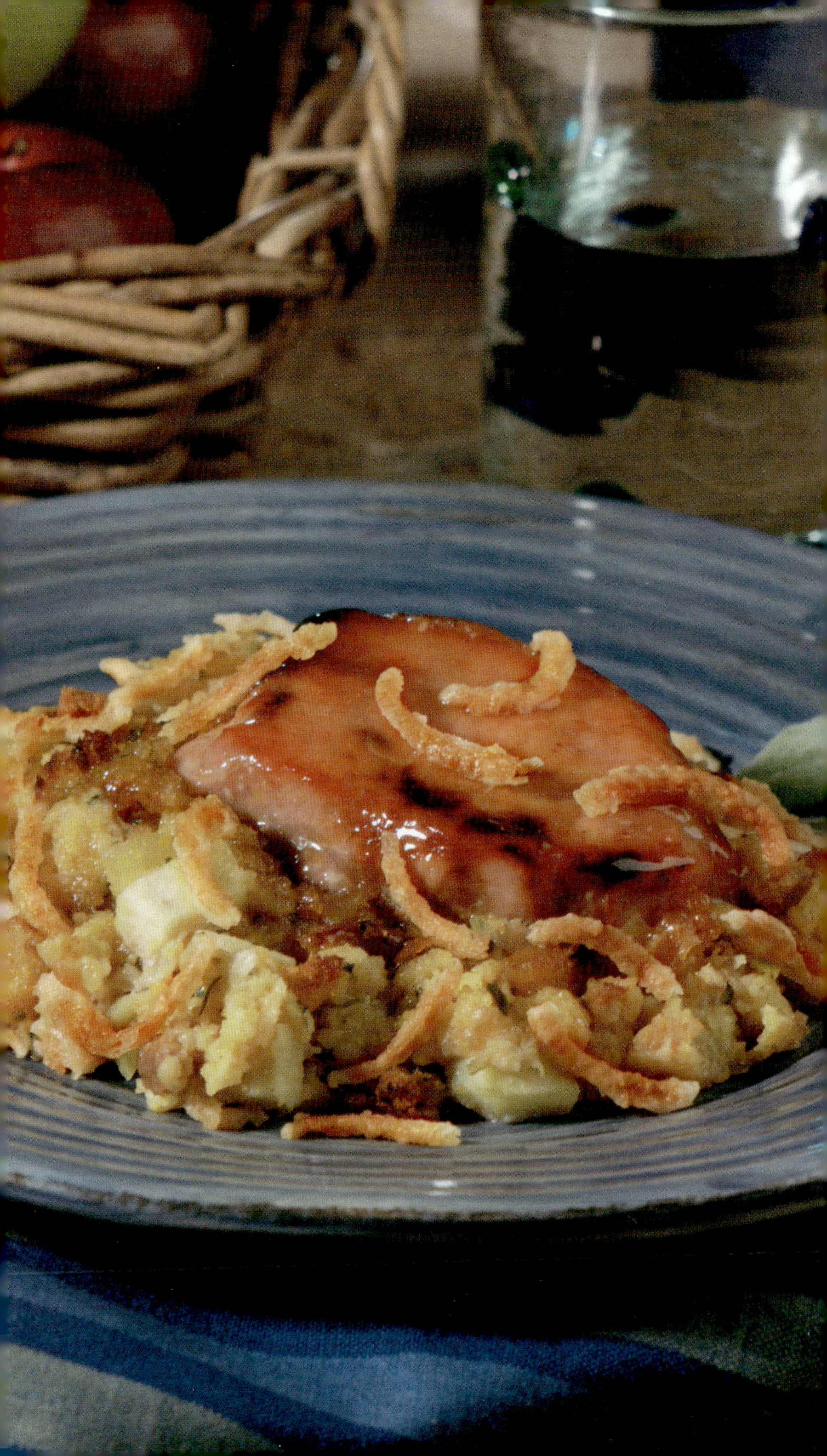

Casseroles

Potato Sausage Casserole

1 pound bulk pork sausage or ground pork
1 can (10 $3/4$ ounces) condensed cream of mushroom soup, undiluted
$3/4$ cup milk
$1/2$ cup chopped onion
$1/2$ teaspoon salt
$1/4$ teaspoon black pepper
3 cups sliced potatoes
$1/2$ tablespoon butter, cut into small pieces
$1^{1}/_{2}$ cups (6 ounces) shredded Cheddar cheese

1. Preheat oven to 350°F. Spray $1^{1}/_{2}$-quart casserole with nonstick cooking spray; set aside.

2. Brown sausage in large skillet over medium-high heat, stirring to separate meat, until no longer pink. Drain fat.

3. Stir together soup, milk, onion, salt and pepper in medium bowl.

4. Place half of potatoes in prepared casserole. Top with half of soup mixture and half of sausage. Repeat layers, ending with sausage. Dot with butter.

5. Cover casserole with foil. Bake $1^{1}/_{4}$ to $1^{1}/_{2}$ hours or until potatoes are tender. Uncover; sprinkle with cheese. Bake until cheese is melted and bubbly.

Makes 6 servings

Potato Sausage Casserole

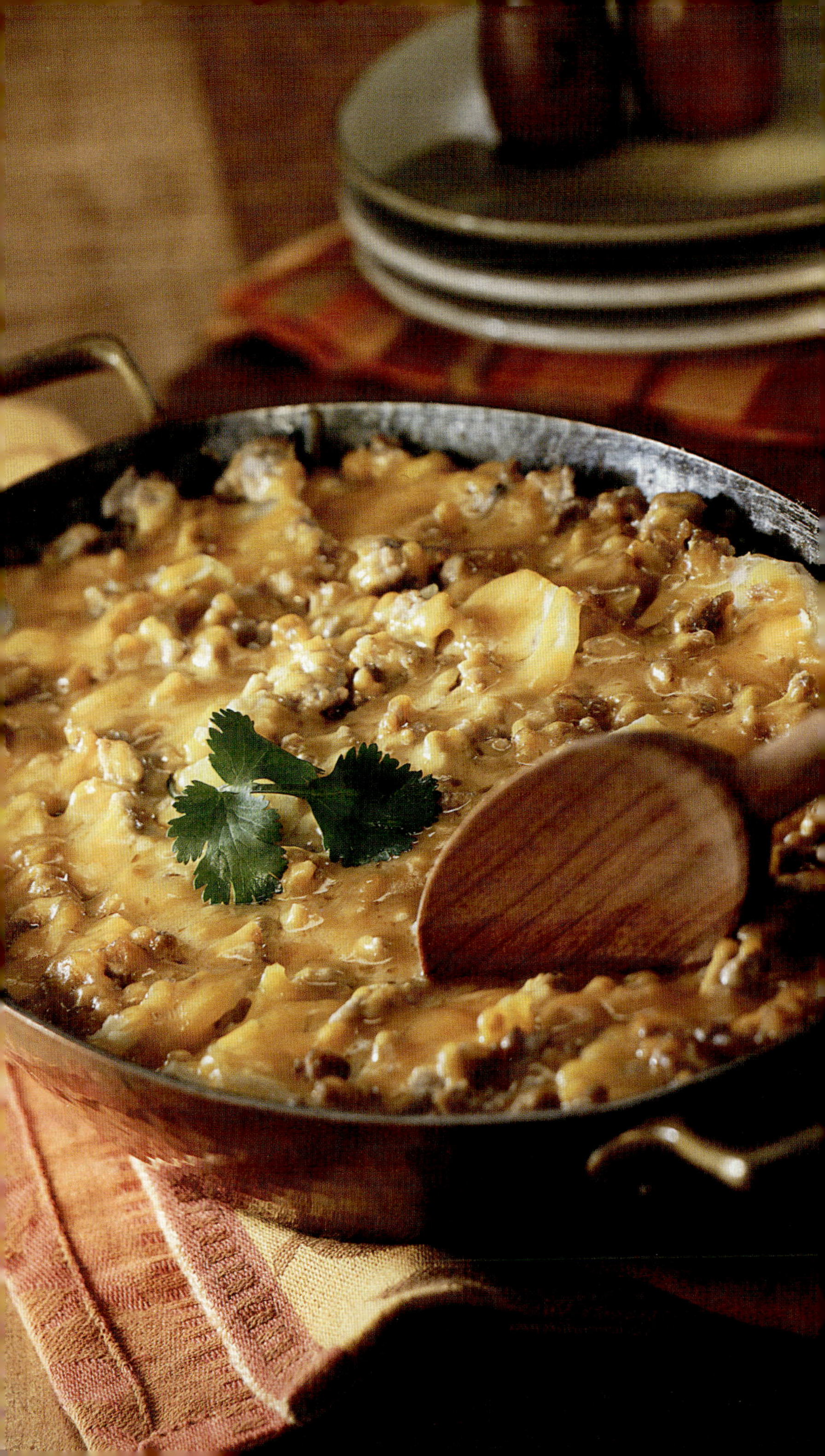

Casseroles

Classic Macaroni and Cheese

   2 cups uncooked elbow macaroni
   3 tablespoons butter or margarine
   1/4 cup chopped onion (optional)
   2 tablespoons all-purpose flour
   1/2 teaspoon salt
   1/8 teaspoon pepper
   2 cups milk
   2 cups (8 ounces) SARGENTO® Chef Style or Fancy Mild Cheddar Shredded Cheese, divided

Cook macaroni according to package directions; drain. In medium saucepan, melt butter and, if desired, cook onion about 5 minutes or until tender. Stir in flour, salt and pepper. Gradually add milk and cook, stirring occasionally, until thickened. Remove from heat. Add 1 1/2 cups cheese and stir until cheese melts. Combine cheese sauce with cooked macaroni. Place in 1 1/2-quart casserole; top with remaining 1/2 cup cheese. Bake at 350°F 30 minutes or until bubbly and cheese is golden brown.   *Makes 6 servings*

Tip: Cooking the flour mixture (also known as a roux) for 1 to 2 minutes before adding milk helps to eliminate the raw taste of flour in the finished cheese sauce.

Casseroles

Chicken Rice Casserole

2 tablespoons MRS. DASH® Minced Onion Medley
2 cups 2% milk
¼ cup butter
2 tablespoons all-purpose flour
1 can (7 ounces) sliced mushrooms, drained or
   1 cup sliced fresh mushrooms
¼ cup chopped fresh parsley
3 cups cooked rice
2 cups cubed cooked chicken or turkey
½ cup diced cooked ham
2 cups coarsely chopped cooked broccoli

Preheat oven to 350°F. Combine Mrs. Dash Minced Onion Medley and milk in a small saucepan or 2-cup glass microwavable measuring cup. Heat just until warm. Melt butter in a large nonstick skillet over medium heat. Whisk in flour. Gradually whisk in milk mixture and heat until thickened; whisk constantly. Remove from heat and stir in mushrooms and parsley. Spray a square glass 2-quart baking dish with nonstick coating spray. Layer rice, chicken, ham and broccoli in prepared dish. Pour sauce evenly over layered ingredients. Bake at 350°F for 25 to 30 minutes or until heated thoroughly.   Makes 8 servings

Prep Time: 10 minutes
Cook Time: 30 minutes

Casseroles

Chicken, Asparagus & Mushroom Bake

1 tablespoon butter
1 tablespoon olive oil
2 boneless skinless chicken breasts (about ½ pound), cut into bite-size pieces
2 cloves garlic, minced
1 cup sliced mushrooms
2 cups sliced asparagus
Black pepper
1 package (about 6 ounces) corn bread stuffing mix
¼ cup dry white wine (optional)
1 can (14½ ounces) fat-free reduced-sodium chicken broth
1 can (10½ ounces) condensed low-sodium cream of asparagus or cream of chicken soup, undiluted

1. Preheat oven to 350°F. Heat butter and oil in large skillet until butter is melted. Add chicken and garlic; cook and stir about 3 minutes over medium-high heat until chicken is cooked through. Add mushrooms; cook and stir 2 minutes. Add asparagus; cook and stir about 5 minutes or until asparagus is crisp-tender. Season with pepper.

2. Transfer mixture to 2½-quart casserole or 6 individual casseroles. Top with stuffing mix.

3. Add wine to skillet, if desired; cook and stir 1 minute over medium-high heat, scraping up any browned bits from bottom of skillet. Add broth and soup; cook and stir until well blended.

4. Pour broth mixture into casserole; mix well. Bake, uncovered, about 35 minutes (30 minutes for individual casseroles) or until heated through and lightly browned. *Makes 6 servings*

Chicken, Asparagus & Mushroom Bake

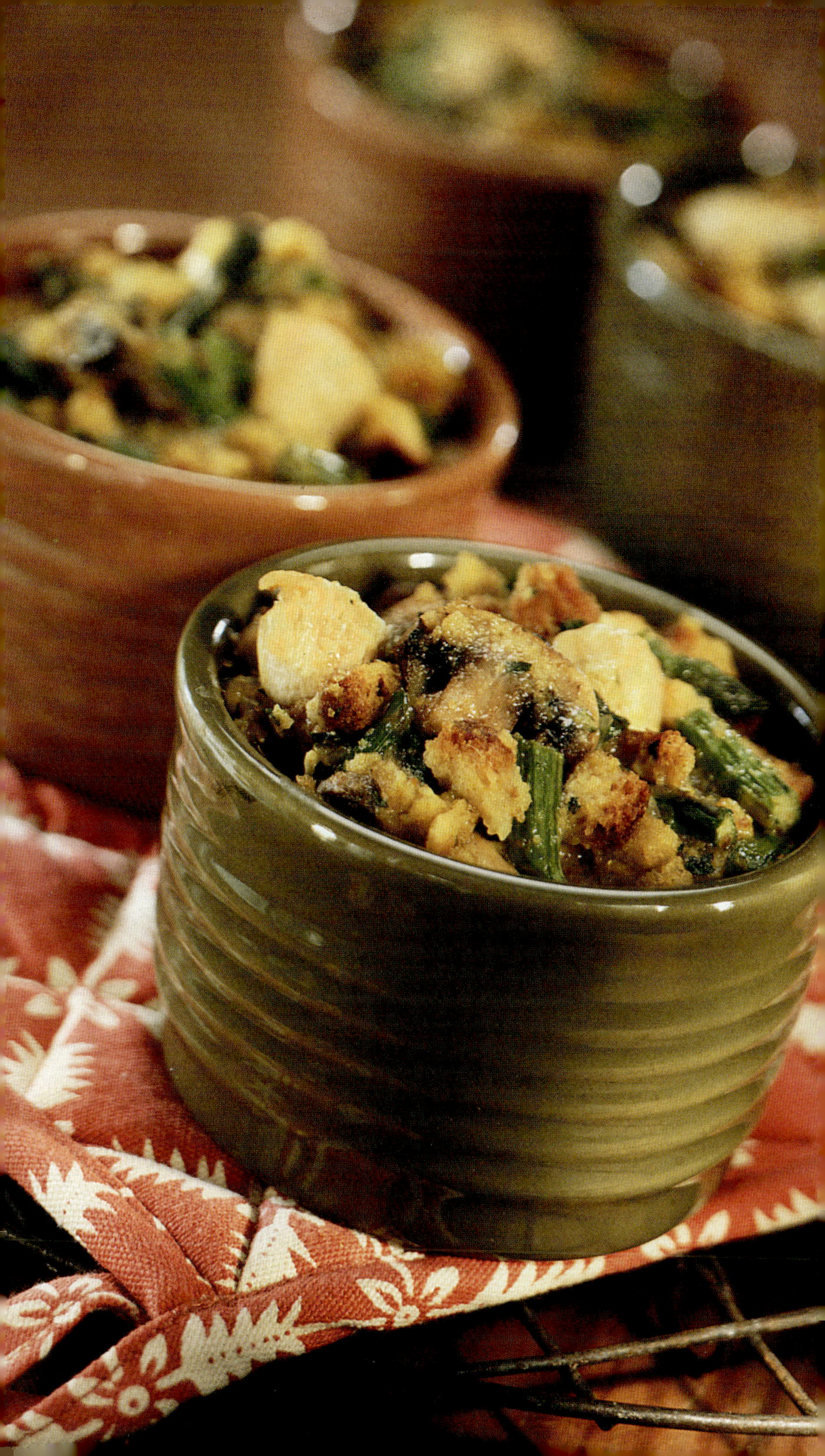

Beef Stroganoff Casserole

1 pound lean ground beef
1/4 teaspoon salt
1/8 teaspoon black pepper
1 teaspoon vegetable oil
8 ounces sliced mushrooms
1 large onion, chopped
3 cloves garlic, minced
1/4 cup beef broth
1 can (10 3/4 ounces) condensed cream of mushroom soup, undiluted
1/2 cup sour cream
1 tablespoon Dijon mustard
4 cups cooked egg noodles
Chopped fresh parsley (optional)

1. Preheat oven to 350°F. Spray 13×9-inch baking dish with nonstick cooking spray.

2. Place beef in large skillet; season with salt and pepper. Brown beef over medium-high heat, stirring to separate meat. Drain fat; set aside.

3. Heat oil in same skillet over medium-high heat until hot. Add mushrooms, onion and garlic; cook and stir 2 to 3 minutes or until onion is tender. Add broth. Reduce heat to medium-low and simmer 3 minutes. Remove from heat; stir in soup, sour cream and mustard until well blended. Return beef to skillet.

4. Place noodles in prepared dish. Pour beef mixture over noodles; stir until noodles are well coated. Bake, uncovered, 30 minutes or until heated through. Sprinkle with parsley.   Makes 6 servings

Beef Stroganoff Casserole

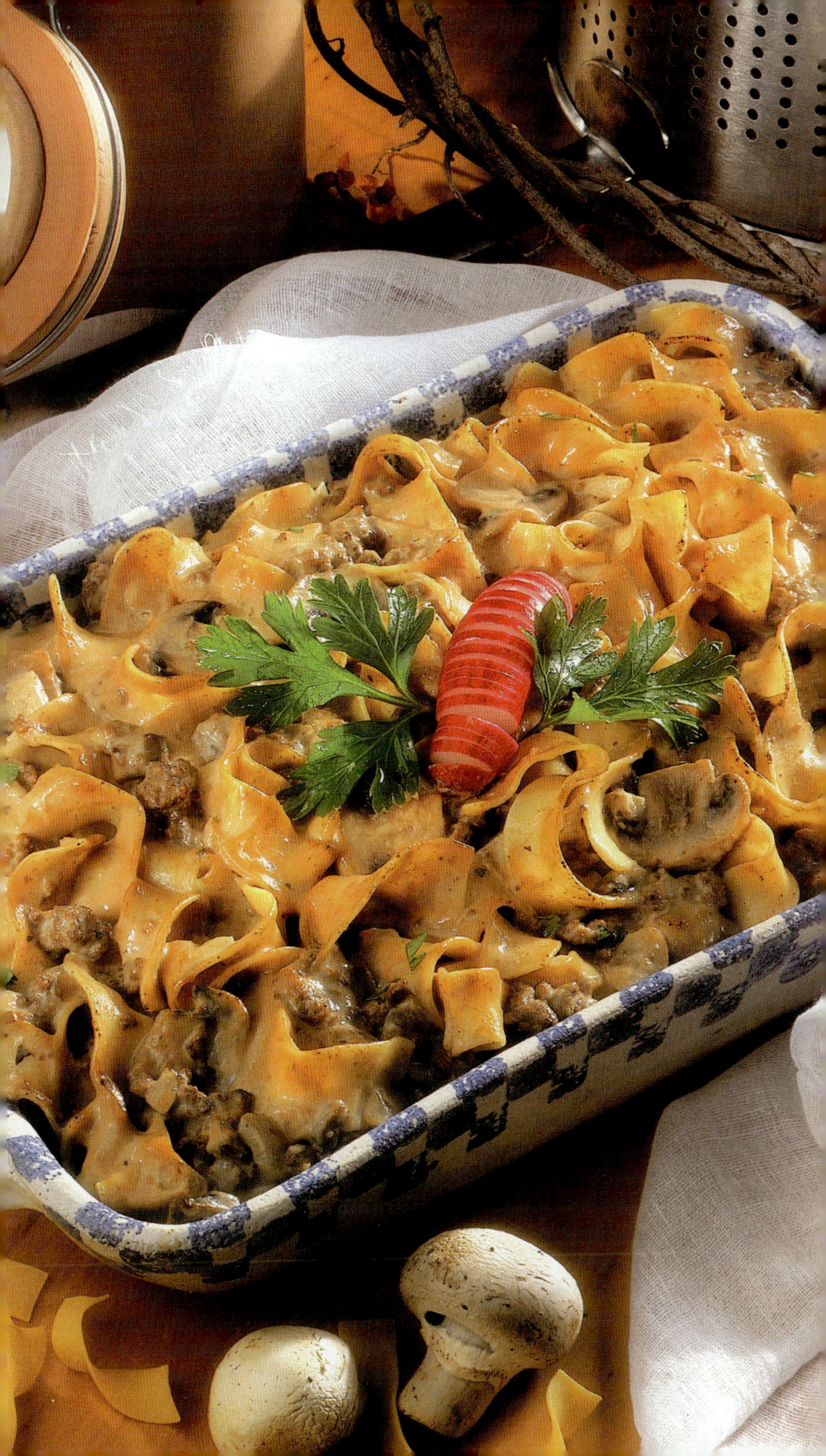

Casseroles

Oven-Baked Stew

2 pounds boneless beef chuck or round steak, cut into 1-inch cubes
1/4 cup all-purpose flour
1 1/3 cups sliced carrots
1 can (14 to 16 ounces) whole peeled tomatoes, undrained and chopped
1 envelope LIPTON® RECIPE SECRETS® Onion Soup Mix*
1/2 cup dry red wine or water
1 cup fresh or canned sliced mushrooms
1 package (8 ounces) medium or broad egg noodles, cooked and drained

Also terrific with LIPTON® RECIPE SECRETS® Beefy Onion, Onion Mushroom or Beefy Mushroom Soup Mix.

1. Preheat oven to 425°F. In 2 1/2-quart shallow casserole, toss beef with flour, then bake uncovered 20 minutes, stirring once.

2. Reduce heat to 350°F. Stir in carrots, tomatoes, soup mix and wine.

3. Bake covered 1 1/2 hours or until beef is tender. Stir in mushrooms and bake covered an additional 10 minutes. Serve over hot noodles.

Makes 8 servings

Prep Time: *20 minutes*
Cook Time: *2 hours*

Oven-Baked Stew

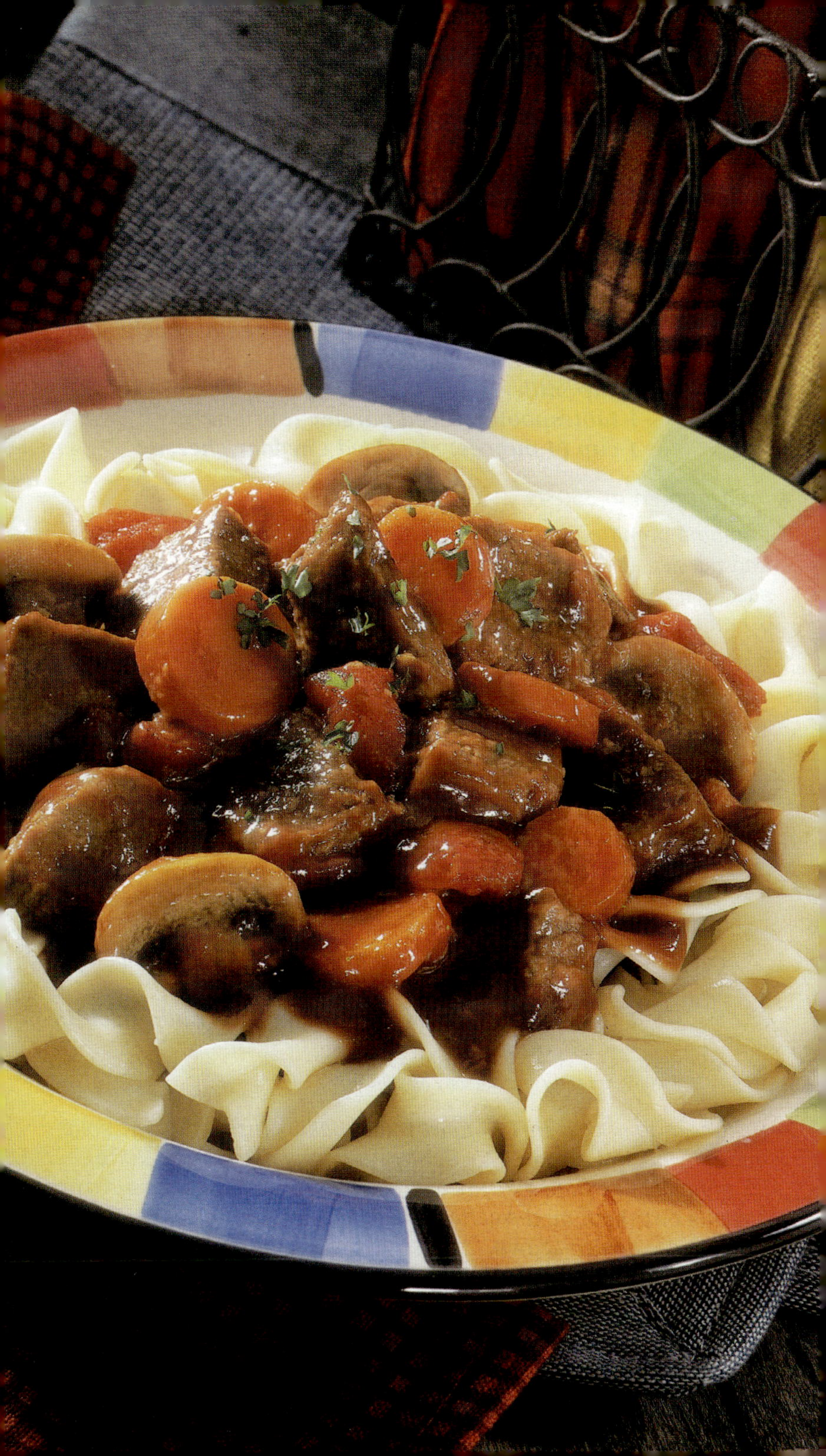

Casseroles

Lit'l Smokies 'n' Macaroni 'n' Cheese

1 package (7 1/4 ounces) macaroni and cheese mix, prepared according to package directions
1 pound HILLSHIRE FARM® Lit'l Smokies
1 can (10 3/4 ounces) condensed cream of celery or mushroom soup, undiluted
1/3 cup milk
1 tablespoon minced parsley (optional)
1 cup (4 ounces) shredded Cheddar cheese

Preheat oven to 350°F.

Combine prepared macaroni and cheese, Lit'l Smokies, soup, milk and parsley, if desired, in medium bowl. Pour into small greased casserole. Sprinkle Cheddar cheese over top. Bake, uncovered, 20 minutes or until heated through.   Makes 8 servings

Ham Pot Pie

1 (10 3/4-ounce) can condensed cream of broccoli soup, undiluted
1/3 cup milk
1/8 teaspoon dried thyme leaves
1/4 teaspoon coarsely ground pepper
2 (5-ounce) cans HORMEL® chunk ham, drained and flaked*
1 (10-ounce) package frozen vegetables, thawed and drained
1 (4 1/2-ounce) can refrigerated buttermilk biscuits (6 count)

*HORMEL® chunk breast of chicken may be substituted here.

Heat oven to 400°F. In 1 1/2-quart round baking dish, combine soup, milk, thyme and pepper. Stir in ham and vegetables. Bake 20 to 25 minutes. Separate biscuits; cut each biscuit into quarters. Arrange biscuits over ham mixture. Bake 12 to 15 minutes longer or until biscuits are golden brown.   Makes 6 servings

Lit'l Smokies 'n' Macaroni 'n' Cheese

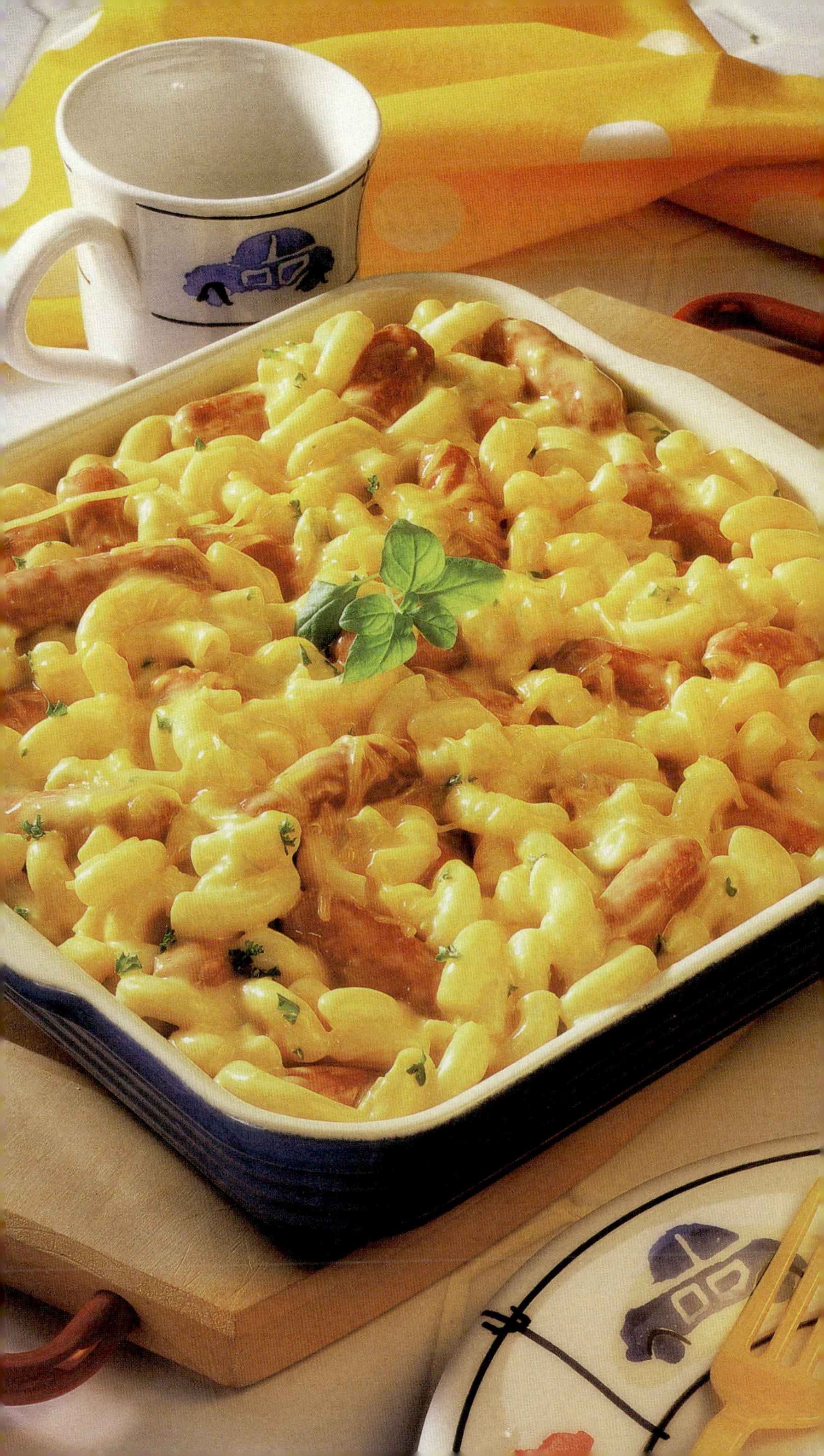

Soups and Salads

Cheddar Broccoli Soup

1 tablespoon olive oil
1 rib celery, chopped (about $^1/_2$ cup)
1 carrot, chopped (about $^1/_2$ cup)
1 small onion, chopped (about $^1/_2$ cup)
$^1/_2$ teaspoon dried thyme leaves, crushed (optional)
2 cans (13$^3/_4$ ounces each) chicken broth
1 jar (1 pound) RAGÚ® Cheese Creations!® Double Cheddar Sauce
1 box (10 ounces) frozen chopped broccoli, thawed and drained

In 3-quart saucepan, heat olive oil over medium heat and cook celery, carrot, onion and thyme 3 minutes or until vegetables are almost tender. Add chicken broth and bring to a boil over high heat. Reduce heat to medium and simmer, uncovered, 10 minutes.

In food processor or blender, purée vegetable mixture until smooth; return to saucepan. Stir in Ragú Cheese Creations! Double Cheddar Sauce and broccoli. Cook 10 minutes or until heated through.

Makes 6 (1-cup) servings

Cheddar Broccoli Soup

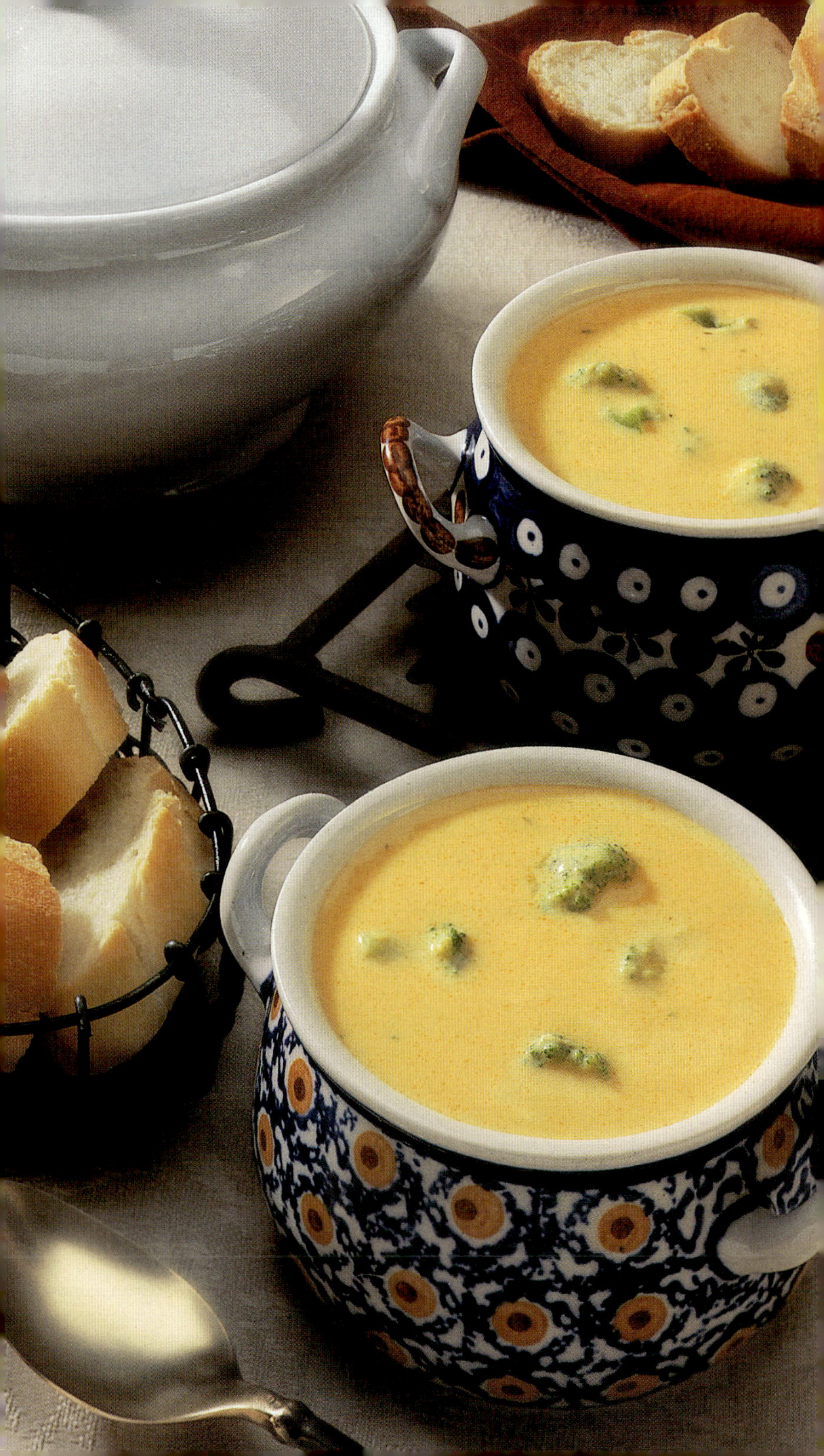

Soups and Salads

Country Chicken Chowder

1 pound chicken tenders
2 tablespoons butter or margarine
1 small onion, chopped
1 stalk celery, sliced
1 small carrot, sliced
1 can (10 3/4 ounces) condensed cream of potato soup, undiluted
1 cup milk
1 cup frozen corn
1/2 teaspoon dried dill weed

1. Cut chicken tenders into 1/2-inch pieces.
2. Melt butter in large saucepan over medium-high heat. Add chicken; cook and stir 5 minutes.
3. Add onion, celery and carrot; cook and stir 3 minutes. Stir in soup, milk, corn and dill; reduce heat to low. Cook about 8 minutes or until corn is tender and chowder is heated through. Add salt and pepper to taste.

Makes 4 servings

Tip: For a special touch, garnish soup with croutons and fresh dill. For a hearty winter meal, serve the chowder in hollowed-out toasted French rolls or small round sourdough loaves.

Prep and Cook Time: 30 minutes

Country Chicken Chowder

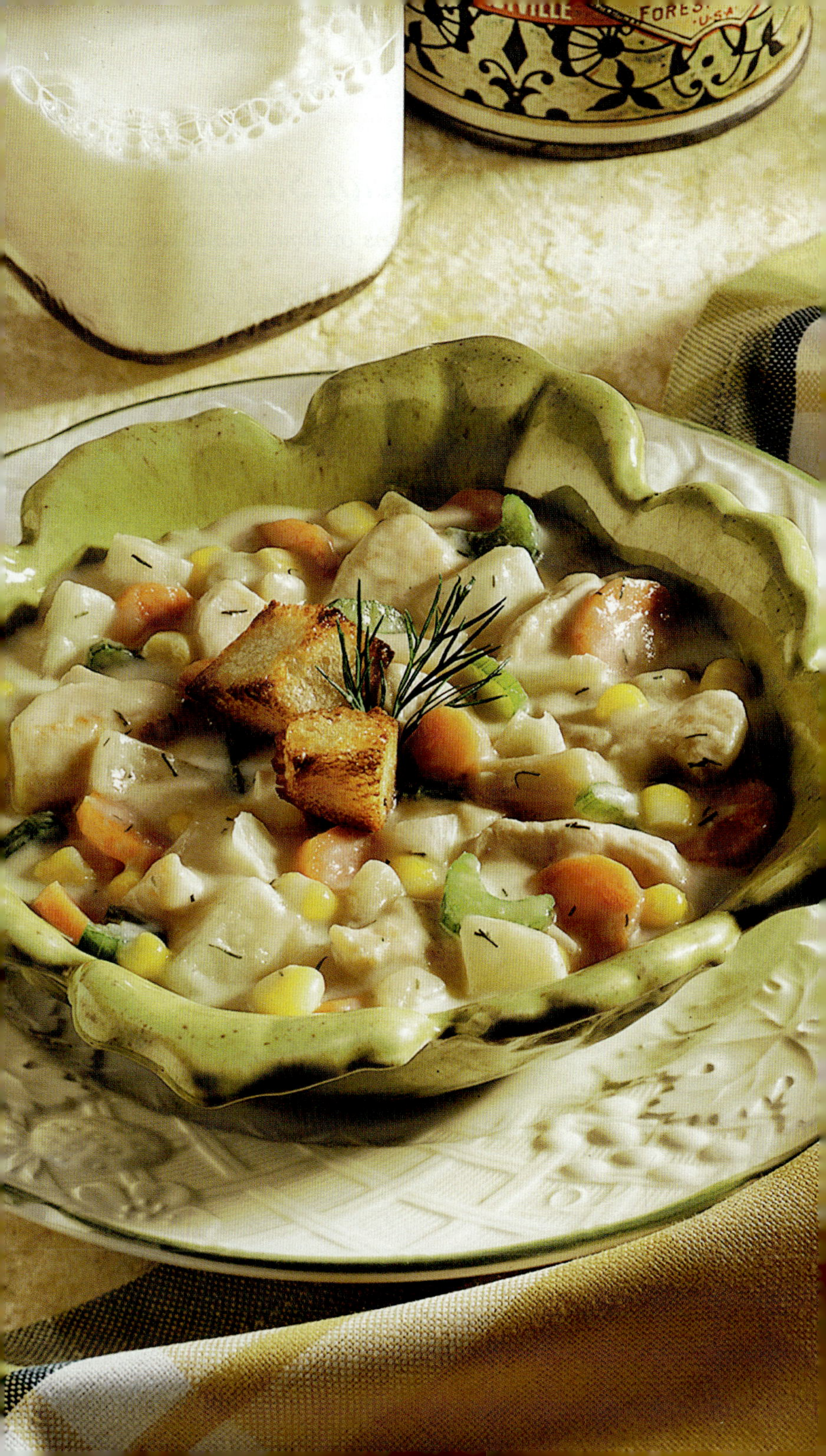

Soups and Salads

Country Bean Soup

1¼ cups dried navy beans or lima beans, rinsed and drained
4 ounces salt pork or fully cooked ham, chopped
¼ cup chopped onion
½ teaspoon dried oregano
¼ teaspoon salt
¼ teaspoon ground ginger
¼ teaspoon dried sage
¼ teaspoon black pepper
2 cups fat-free (skim) milk
2 tablespoons butter

1. Place navy beans in large saucepan; add enough water to cover beans. Bring to a boil; reduce heat and simmer 2 minutes. Remove from heat; cover and let stand for 1 hour. (Or cover beans with water and soak overnight.)

2. Drain beans and return to saucepan. Stir in 2½ cups water, salt pork, onion, oregano, salt, ginger, sage and pepper. Bring to a boil; reduce heat. Cover and simmer 2 to 2½ hours or until beans are tender. (If necessary, add more water during cooking.) Add milk and butter, stirring until mixture is heated through and butter is melted. Season with additional salt and pepper, if desired.

Makes 6 servings

Country Bean Soup

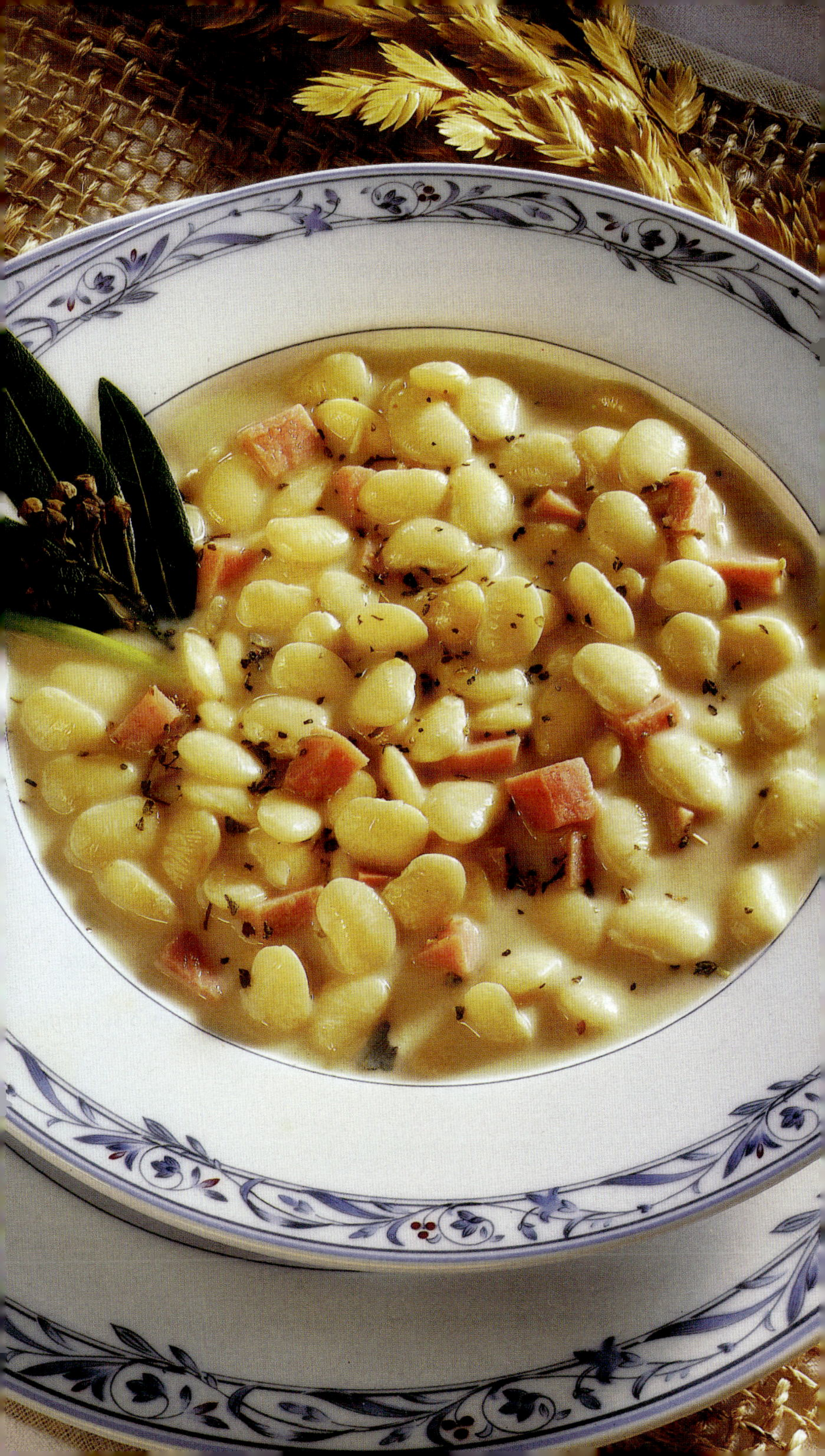

Soups and Salads

Pork and Cabbage Soup

1/2 pound pork loin, cut into 1/2-inch cubes
1 medium onion, chopped
2 strips bacon, finely chopped
2 cups canned chicken broth
2 cups canned beef broth
1 can (28 ounces) tomatoes, cut-up and drained
2 medium carrots, sliced
3/4 teaspoon dried marjoram leaves
1 bay leaf
1/8 teaspoon black pepper
1/4 medium cabbage, chopped
2 tablespoons chopped fresh parsley
Additional chopped fresh parsley

1. Cook and stir pork, onion and bacon in 5-quart Dutch oven over medium heat until meat loses its pink color and onion is slightly tender. Remove from heat. Drain fat.

2. Stir in chicken and beef broth. Stir in tomatoes, carrots, marjoram, bay leaf and pepper. Bring to a boil over high heat. Reduce heat to medium-low; simmer, uncovered, about 30 minutes. Remove and discard bay leaf. Skim off fat.

3. Stir cabbage into soup. Bring to a boil over high heat. Reduce heat to medium-low; simmer, uncovered, about 15 minutes or until cabbage is tender.

4. Remove soup from heat; stir in 2 tablespoons parsley. Ladle into bowls. Garnish each serving with additional parsley.

Makes 6 servings

Soups and Salads

German Potato Salad

    4 cups sliced peeled Colorado potatoes
    4 slices bacon
    ¾ cup chopped onion
    ¼ cup sugar
    3 tablespoons all-purpose flour
1½ teaspoons salt
    1 teaspoon celery seeds
    ¼ teaspoon black pepper
    1 cup water
    ¾ cup vinegar
    2 hard-cooked eggs, chopped

Cook potatoes in boiling water until tender; drain. Meanwhile, cook bacon in medium skillet until crisp. Drain on paper towels; cool and crumble. Cook and stir onion in drippings until tender. Combine sugar, flour, salt, celery seeds and pepper; blend in water and vinegar. Stir into onion in skillet; heat until bubbly. Pour over combined potatoes, bacon and eggs; toss. Serve immediately.

Makes 6 servings

Favorite recipe from **Colorado Potato Administrative Committee**

Inside-Out Egg Salad

    6 hard-cooked eggs, peeled
    ⅓ cup mayonnaise
    ¼ cup chopped celery
    1 tablespoon French's® Classic Yellow® Mustard

1. Cut eggs in half lengthwise. Remove egg yolks. Combine yolks, mayonnaise, celery and mustard in small bowl. Add salt and pepper to taste.

2. Spoon egg yolk mixture into egg whites. Sprinkle with paprika, if desired. Chill before serving.

Makes 12 servings

Prep Time: 20 minutes

Veg•All® Italian Soup

2 tablespoons butter
1 cup diced onion
1 cup shredded cabbage
2 cups water
2 cans (14½ ounces each) stewed tomatoes
1 can (15 ounces) VEG•ALL® Original Mixed Vegetables, drained
1 tablespoon chopped fresh parsley
½ teaspoon dried basil
½ teaspoon dried oregano
½ teaspoon black pepper

In large saucepan, melt butter. Stir in onion and cabbage. Heat for 2 minutes. Add water; cover and simmer for 10 minutes. Stir in tomatoes, Veg•All and seasonings. Simmer for 10 minutes.

Makes 6 servings

Easy Chicken Salad

¼ cup finely diced celery
¼ cup reduced-fat mayonnaise
2 tablespoons sweet pickle relish
1 tablespoon minced onion
½ teaspoon Dijon mustard
⅛ teaspoon salt
Black pepper
2 cups cubed cooked chicken
Salad greens

1. *Combine celery, mayonnaise, relish, onion, mustard, salt and pepper in medium bowl; mix well. Stir in chicken. Cover and refrigerate at least 1 hour.*

2. *Serve on salad greens with fruit, if desired.*   *Makes 2 servings*

Veg•All® Italian Soup

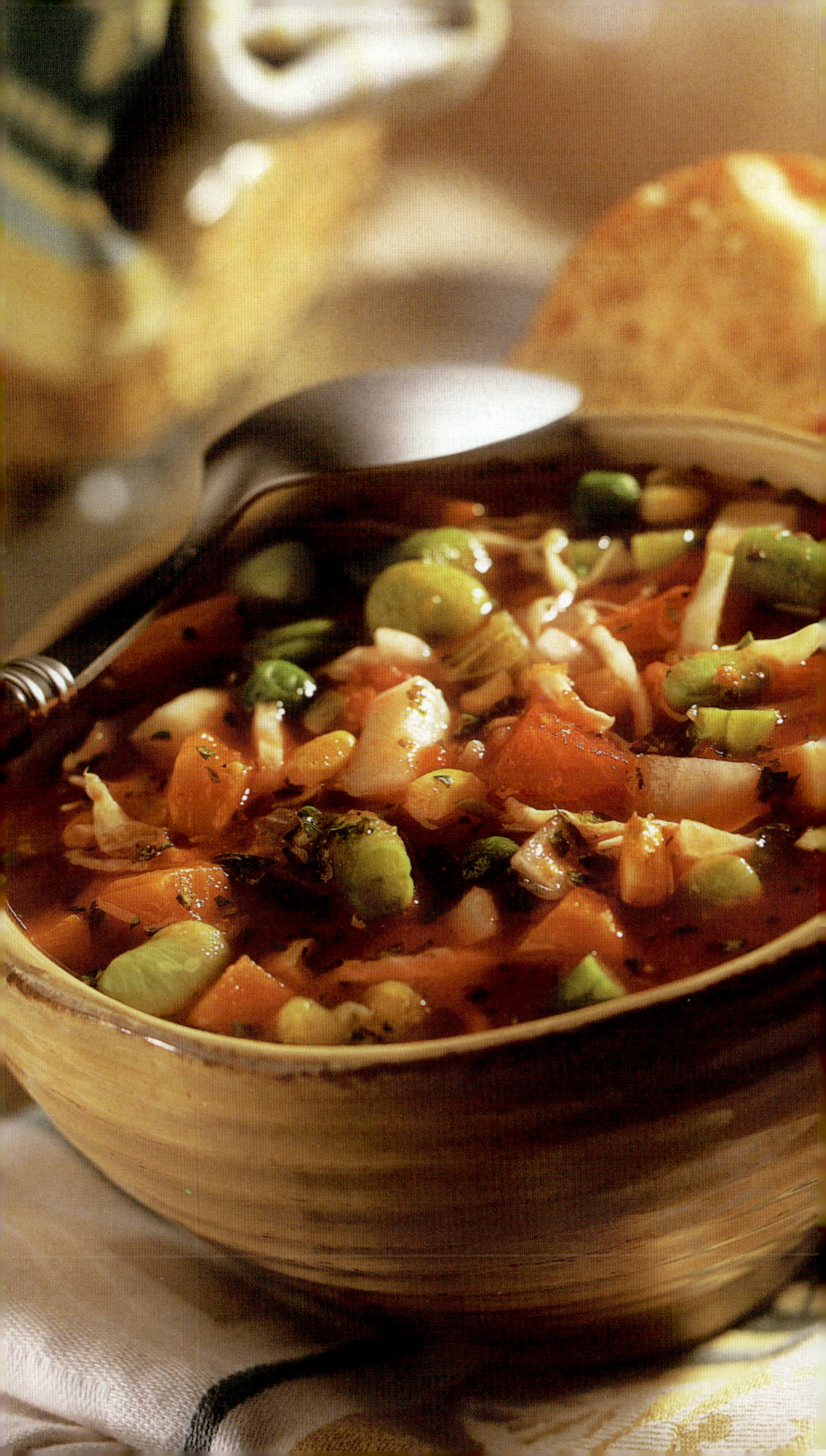

Soups and Salads

Parsley, Ham and Pasta Salad

> 2 cups uncooked elbow macaroni
> 2 cups (12 ounces) CURE 81® ham, cut into strips
> 1 cup sliced celery
> ½ cup sliced green onions
> 1 cup mayonnaise or salad dressing
> 1 cup packed fresh parsley, finely chopped
> ¼ cup grated Parmesan cheese
> ¼ cup white wine vinegar
> 1 clove garlic, minced

Cook macaroni according to package directions. In large bowl, combine ham, macaroni, celery and green onions. In small bowl, combine mayonnaise, parsley, cheese, vinegar and garlic; toss with pasta. Cover and refrigerate 1 to 2 hours to blend flavors.

Makes 6 to 8 servings

Cheeseburger Soup

> ½ pound ground beef
> 3½ cups water
> ½ cup cherry tomato halves or chopped tomato
> 1 pouch LIPTON® Soup Secrets Ring-O-Noodle Soup Mix with Real Chicken Broth
> 1 cup (4 ounces) Cheddar cheese, shredded

Shape ground beef into 16 mini burgers.

In large saucepan, thoroughly brown burgers; drain. Add water, tomatoes and soup mix; bring to a boil. Reduce heat and simmer uncovered, stirring occasionally, 5 minutes or until burgers are cooked and noodles are tender. Stir in cheese.

Makes about 4 (1-cup) servings

Parsley, Ham and Pasta Salad

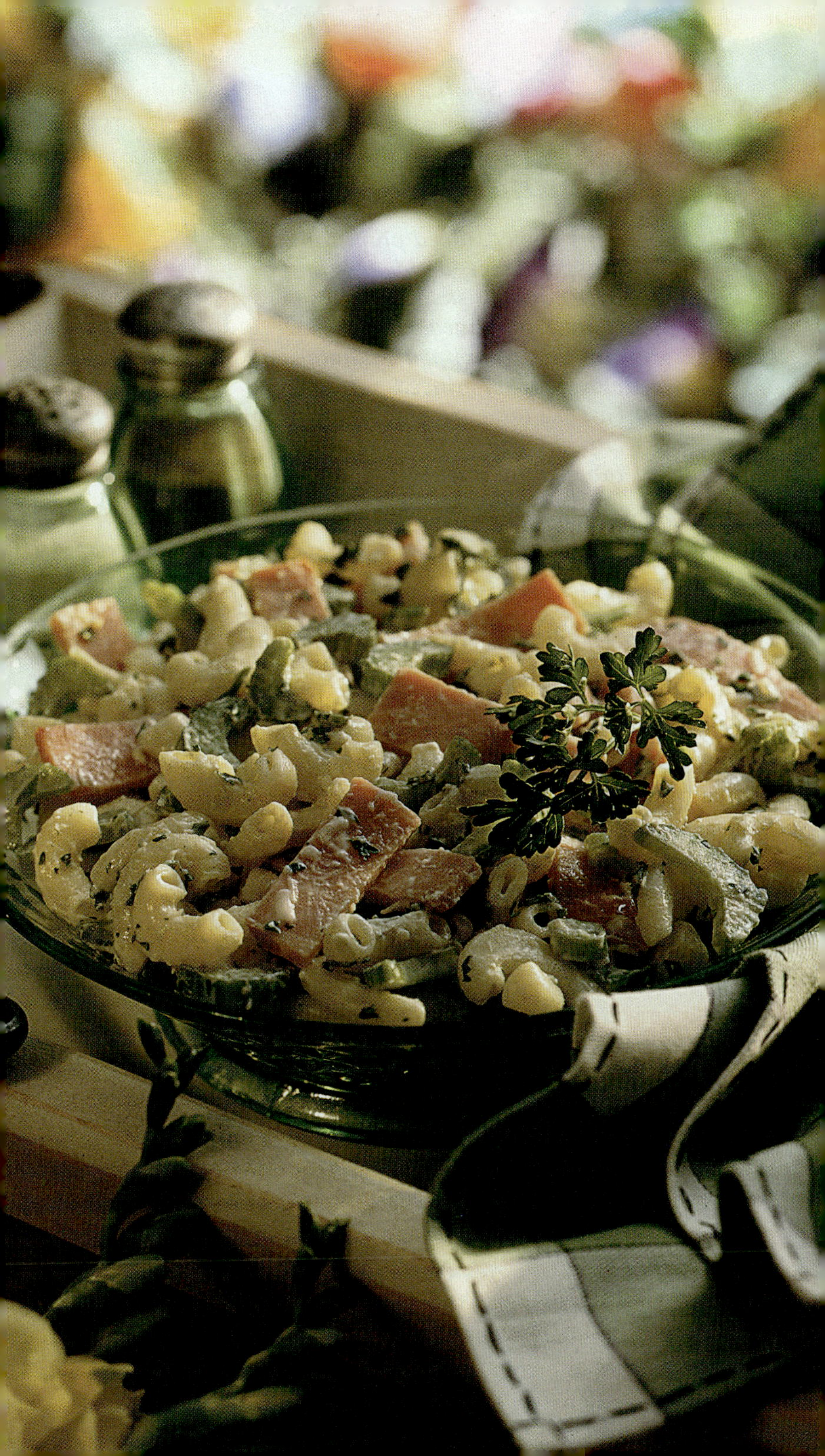

Soups and Salads

Corn and Tomato Chowder

1½ cups peeled, diced plum tomatoes
¾ teaspoon salt, divided
2 ears corn, husks removed
1 tablespoon margarine
½ cup finely chopped shallots
1 clove garlic, minced
1 can (12 ounces) evaporated skimmed milk
1 cup chicken broth
1 tablespoon finely chopped fresh sage or
   1 teaspoon rubbed sage
¼ teaspoon black pepper
1 tablespoon cornstarch
2 tablespoons cold water

1. Place tomatoes in nonmetal colander over bowl. Sprinkle with ½ teaspoon salt; toss to mix well. Allow tomatoes to drain at least 1 hour.

2. Meanwhile, cut corn kernels off cobs into small bowl. Scrape cobs with dull side of knife blade to extract liquid; set aside. Discard 1 cob; break remaining cob in half.

3. Heat margarine in heavy medium saucepan over medium-high heat until melted and bubbly. Add shallots and garlic; reduce heat to low. Cover and cook about 5 minutes or until shallots are soft and translucent. Add evaporated milk, broth, sage, pepper and reserved corn cob halves. Bring to a boil over high heat. Reduce heat to low; simmer, uncovered, 10 minutes. Remove and discard cob halves.

4. Add corn with liquid; return to a boil over medium-high heat. Reduce heat to low; simmer, uncovered, 15 minutes more. Stir cornstarch into water until smooth; add to chowder, mixing well. Cook and stir until thickened. Remove from heat; stir in drained tomatoes and remaining ¼ teaspoon salt. Spoon into bowls. Garnish with additional fresh sage, if desired.   *Makes 4 servings*

Corn and Tomato Chowder

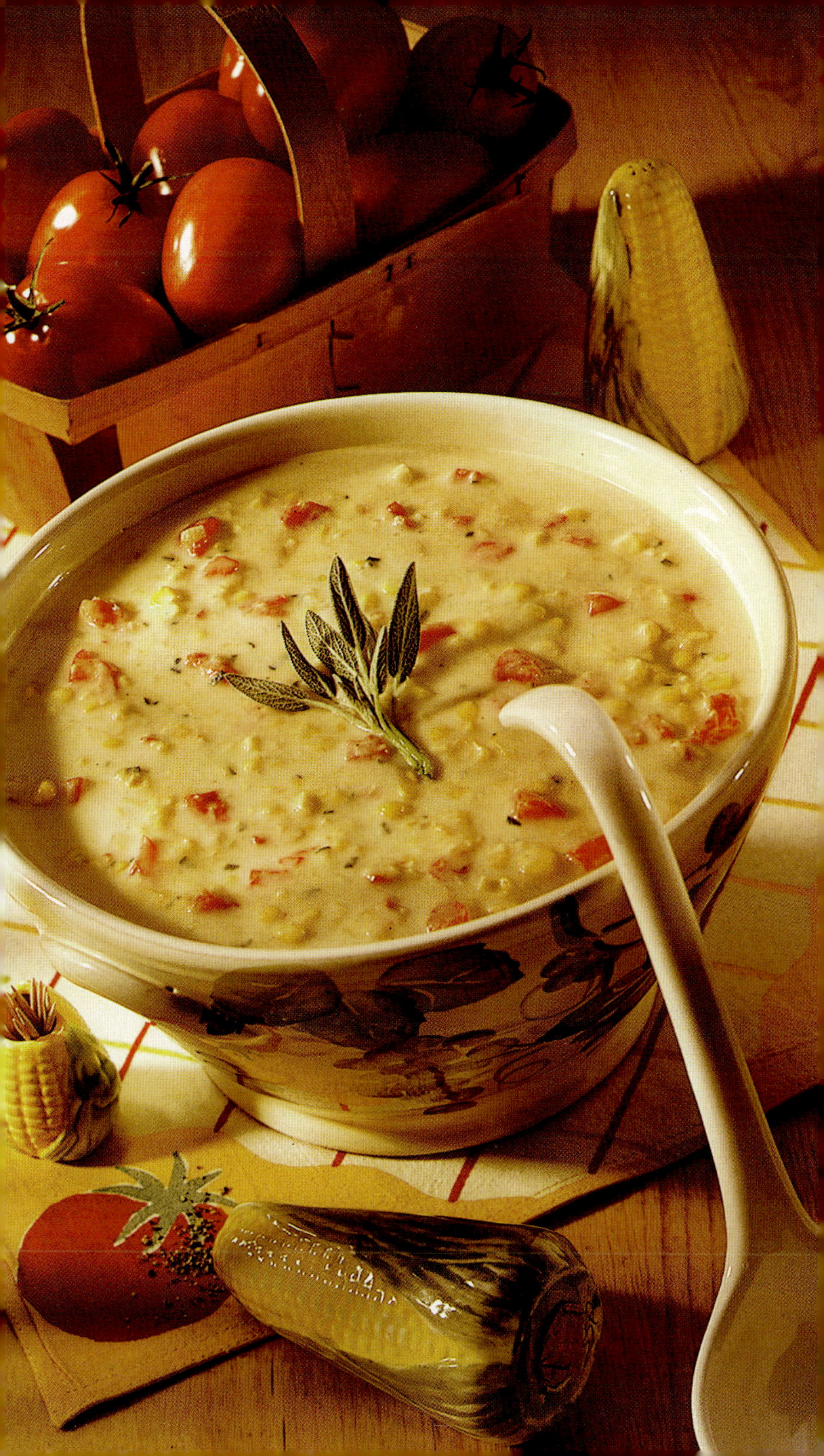

Side Dishes

Savory Skillet Broccoli

1 tablespoon BERTOLLI® Olive Oil
6 cups fresh broccoli florets or 1 pound green beans, trimmed
1 envelope LIPTON® RECIPE SECRETS® Golden Onion Soup Mix*
1½ cups water

*Also terrific with LIPTON® RECIPE SECRETS® Onion Mushroom Soup Mix.

1. In 12-inch skillet, heat oil over medium-high heat and cook broccoli, stirring occasionally, 2 minutes.

2. Stir in soup mix blended with water. Bring to a boil over high heat.

3. Reduce heat to medium-low and simmer covered 6 minutes or until broccoli is tender.

Makes 4 servings

Prep Time: 5 minutes
Cook Time: 10 minutes

Savory Skillet Broccoli

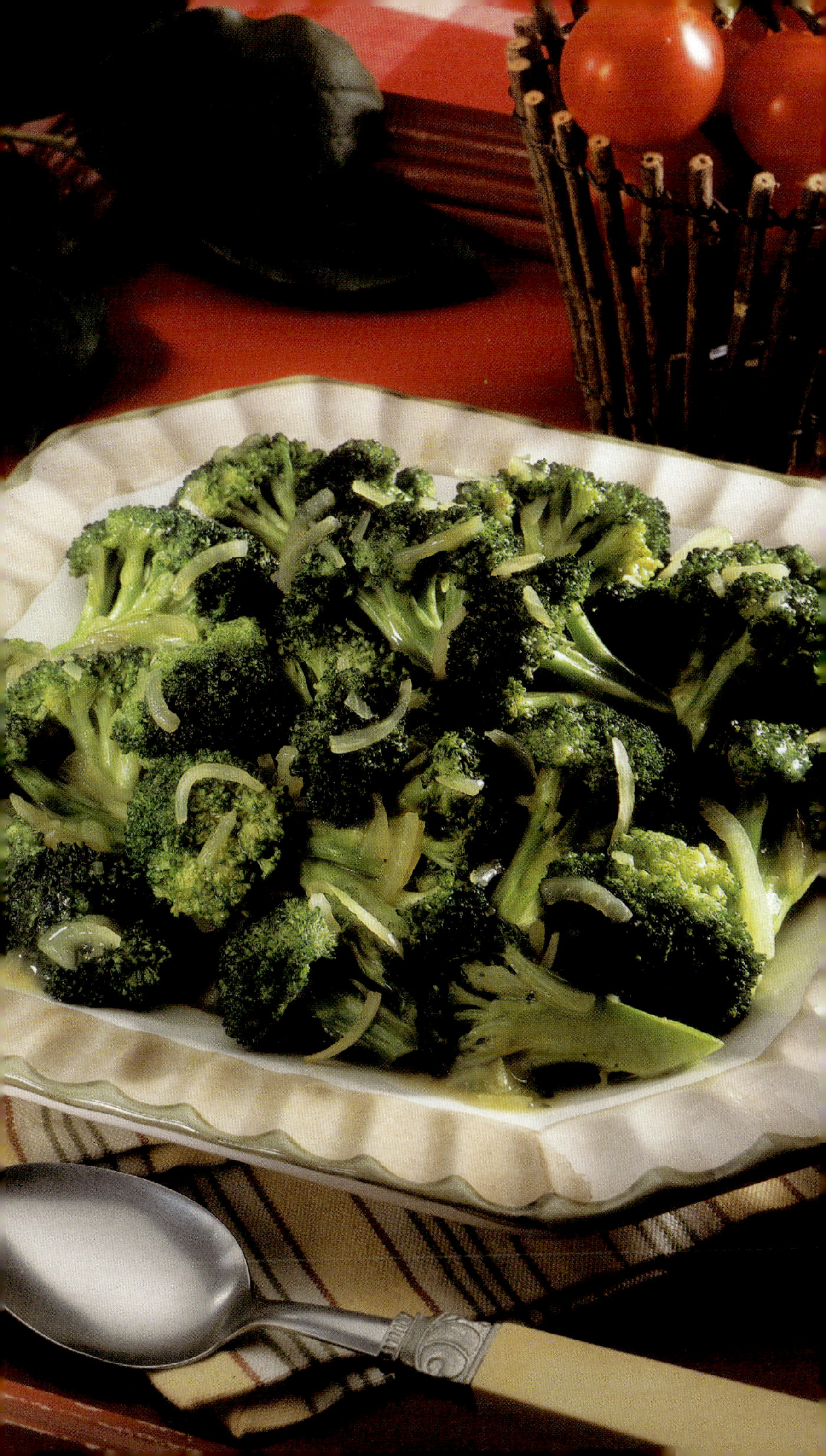

Side Dishes

Bacon and Maple Grits Puff

8 slices bacon
2 cups milk
1¼ cups water
1 cup quick-cooking grits
½ teaspoon salt
½ cup pure maple syrup
4 eggs
Fresh chives (optional)

1. Preheat oven to 350°F. Grease 1½-quart round casserole or soufflé dish; set aside.

2. Cook bacon in large skillet over medium-high heat about 7 minutes or until crisp. Remove bacon to paper towel; set aside. Reserve 2 tablespoons bacon drippings.

3. Combine milk, water, grits and salt in medium saucepan. Bring to a boil over medium heat, stirring frequently. Simmer 2 to 3 minutes or until mixture thickens, stirring constantly. Remove from heat; stir in syrup and reserved 2 tablespoons bacon drippings.

4. Crumble bacon; reserve ¼ cup for garnish. Stir remaining crumbled bacon into grits mixture.

5. Beat eggs in medium bowl. Gradually stir small amount of grits mixture into eggs, then stir back into remaining grits mixture. Pour into prepared casserole.

6. Bake 1 hour and 20 minutes or until knife inserted in center comes out clean. Top with reserved ¼ cup bacon. Garnish with fresh chives, if desired. Serve immediately.   *Makes 6 to 8 servings*

Note: *Puff will fall slightly after removing from oven.*

Bacon and Maple Grits Puff

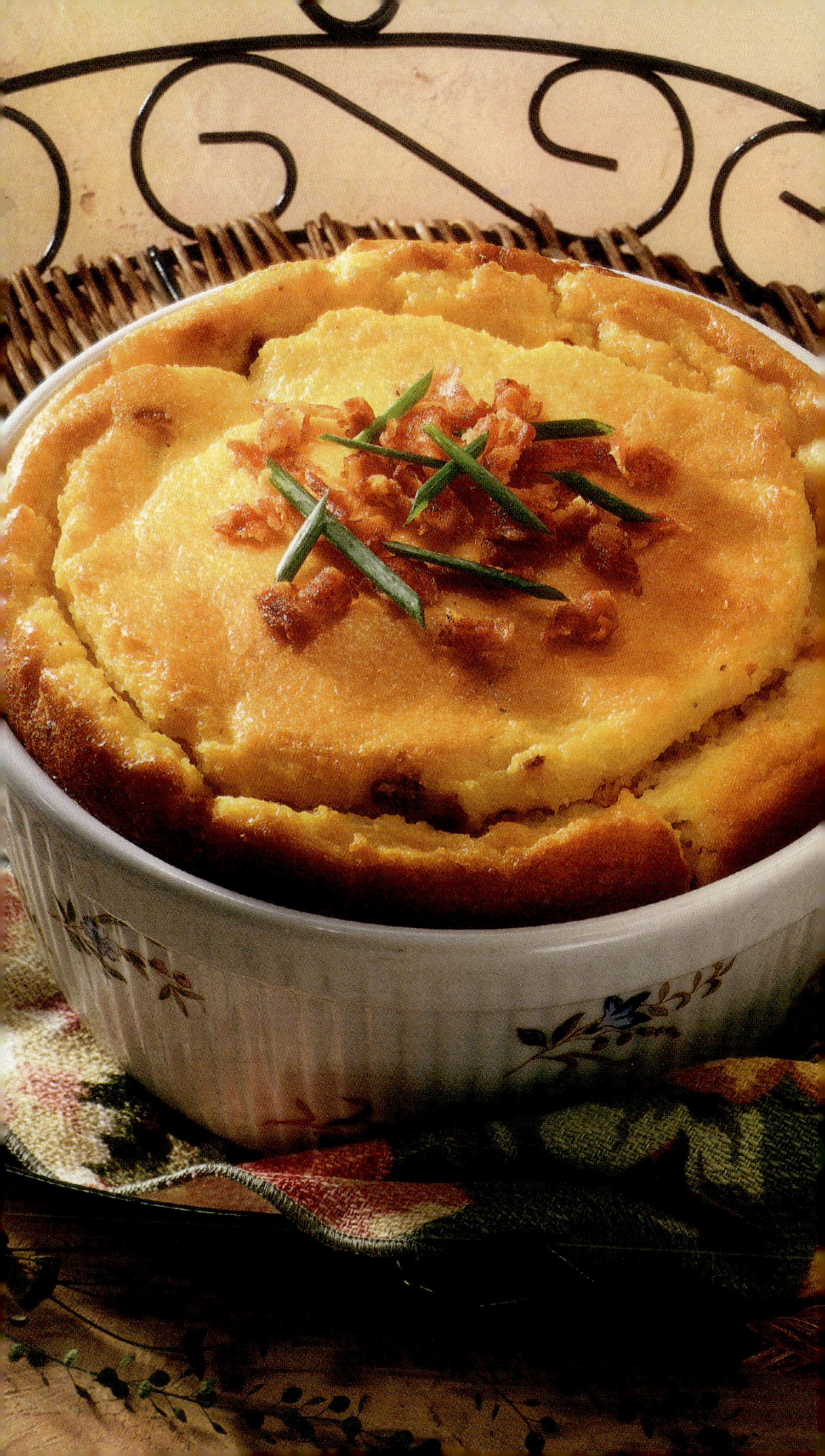

Side Dishes

Festive Cranberry Mold

1/2 cup water
1 package (6 ounces) raspberry-flavored gelatin
1 can (8 ounces) cranberry sauce
1 2/3 cups cranberry juice cocktail
1 cup sliced bananas (optional)
1/2 cup walnuts, toasted (optional)

Bring water to a boil, in medium saucepan over medium-high heat. Add gelatin and stir until dissolved. Fold in cranberry sauce. Reduce heat to medium; cook until sauce is melted. Stir in cranberry juice cocktail.

Refrigerate mixture until slightly thickened. Fold in banana slices and walnuts, if desired. Pour mixture into 4-cup mold; cover and refrigerate until gelatin is set. *Makes 8 servings*

Chunky Applesauce

10 tart apples (about 3 pounds) peeled, cored and chopped
3/4 cup packed light brown sugar
1/2 cup apple juice or apple cider
1 1/2 teaspoons ground cinnamon
1/8 teaspoon salt
1/8 teaspoon ground nutmeg

1. Combine apples, brown sugar, apple juice, cinnamon, salt and nutmeg in heavy, large saucepan; cover. Cook over medium-low heat 40 to 45 minutes or until apples are tender, stirring occasionally. Remove saucepan from heat. Cool completely.

2. Store in airtight container in refrigerator up to 1 month.
Makes about 5 1/2 cups

Festive Cranberry Mold

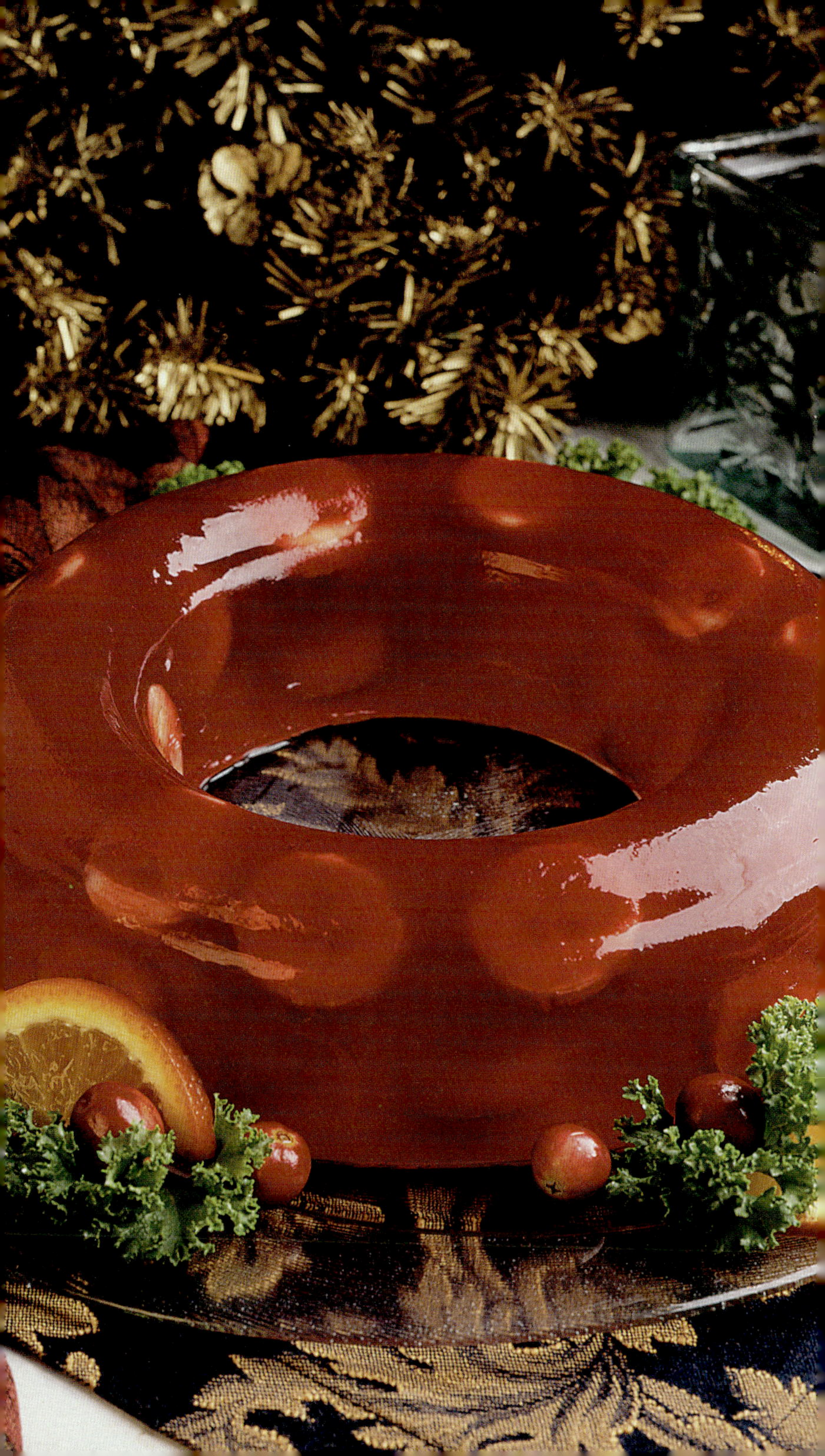

Side Dishes

Golden Corn Pudding

2 tablespoons butter or margarine
3 tablespoons all-purpose flour
1 can (14 3/4 ounces) DEL MONTE® Cream Style Golden Sweet Corn
1/4 cup yellow cornmeal
2 eggs, separated
1 package (3 ounces) cream cheese, softened
1 can (8 3/4 ounces) DEL MONTE Whole Kernel Golden Sweet Corn, drained

1. Preheat oven to 350°F.

2. Melt butter in medium saucepan. Add flour and stir until smooth. Blend in cream style corn and cornmeal. Bring to a boil over medium heat, stirring constantly.

3. Place egg yolks in small bowl; stir in 1/2 cup hot mixture. Pour mixture back into saucepan. Add cream cheese and whole kernel corn.

4. Place egg whites in clean, deep narrow bowl and beat until stiff peaks form. With rubber spatula, gently fold egg whites into corn mixture.

5. Pour mixture into 1 1/2-quart straight-sided baking dish. Bake 30 to 35 minutes or until lightly browned.

Makes 4 to 6 servings

Tip: Pudding can be prepared up to 3 hours ahead of serving time. Cover and refrigerate until about 30 minutes before baking.

Prep Time: 10 minutes
Bake Time: 35 minutes

Side Dishes

Kentucky Cornbread & Sausage Stuffing

1/2 pound BOB EVANS® Original Recipe Roll Sausage
3 cups fresh bread cubes, dried or toasted
3 cups crumbled prepared cornbread
1 large apple, peeled and chopped
1 small onion, chopped
1 cup chicken or turkey broth
2 tablespoons minced fresh parsley
1 teaspoon salt
1 teaspoon rubbed sage or poultry seasoning
1/4 teaspoon black pepper

Crumble sausage into small skillet. Cook over medium heat until browned, stirring occasionally. Place sausage and drippings in large bowl. Add remaining ingredients; toss lightly. Use to stuff chicken loosely just before roasting. Or, place stuffing in greased 13×9-inch baking dish. Add additional broth for more moist stuffing, if desired. Bake in 350°F oven 30 minutes. Leftover stuffing should be removed from bird and stored separately in refrigerator. Reheat thoroughly before serving.

Makes enough stuffing for 5-pound chicken, 8 servings

Sweet Potato Apple Bake

3 cups mashed cooked sweet potatoes
2 to 3 medium apples, peeled, sliced
Ground cinnamon
1/2 cup apple jelly

Preheat oven to 350°F. Spray 9-inch glass pie plate with nonstick cooking spray. Fill dish evenly with mashed sweet potatoes. Arrange apple slices on top. Sprinkle apples with cinnamon. Melt apple jelly over low heat in small saucepan. Brush over apples. Bake 30 minutes or until apples are tender.

Makes 6 servings

Favorite recipe from **New York Apple Association, Inc.**

Swiss-Style Vegetables

3/4 cup cubed unpeeled red potato
2 cups broccoli florets
1 cup cauliflower florets
2 teaspoons margarine
1 cup sliced mushrooms
1 tablespoon all-purpose flour
1 cup half-and-half
1/2 cup (2 ounces) shredded Swiss cheese
1/4 teaspoon salt
1/4 teaspoon black pepper
1/4 teaspoon hot pepper sauce (optional)
1/8 teaspoon ground nutmeg
1/4 cup grated Parmesan cheese

1. Place potato in medium saucepan; cover with cold water. Bring water to a boil. Reduce heat; cover and simmer 10 minutes. Add broccoli and cauliflower; cover and cook about 5 minutes or until all vegetables are tender. Drain; remove vegetables and set aside.

2. Melt margarine in same pan over medium-high heat. Add mushrooms. Cook and stir 2 minutes. Reduce heat; stir in flour; cook 1 minute. Slowly stir in half-and-half; cook and stir until mixture thickens. Remove from heat. Add Swiss cheese, stirring until melted. Stir in salt, pepper, hot pepper sauce, if desired, and nutmeg.

3. Preheat broiler. Spray small shallow casserole with nonstick cooking spray.

4. Arrange vegetables in single layer in prepared casserole. Spoon sauce mixture over vegetables; sprinkle with Parmesan cheese.

5. Heat casserole under broiler about 1 minute or until cheese melts and browns.

Makes 6 (1/2-cup) servings

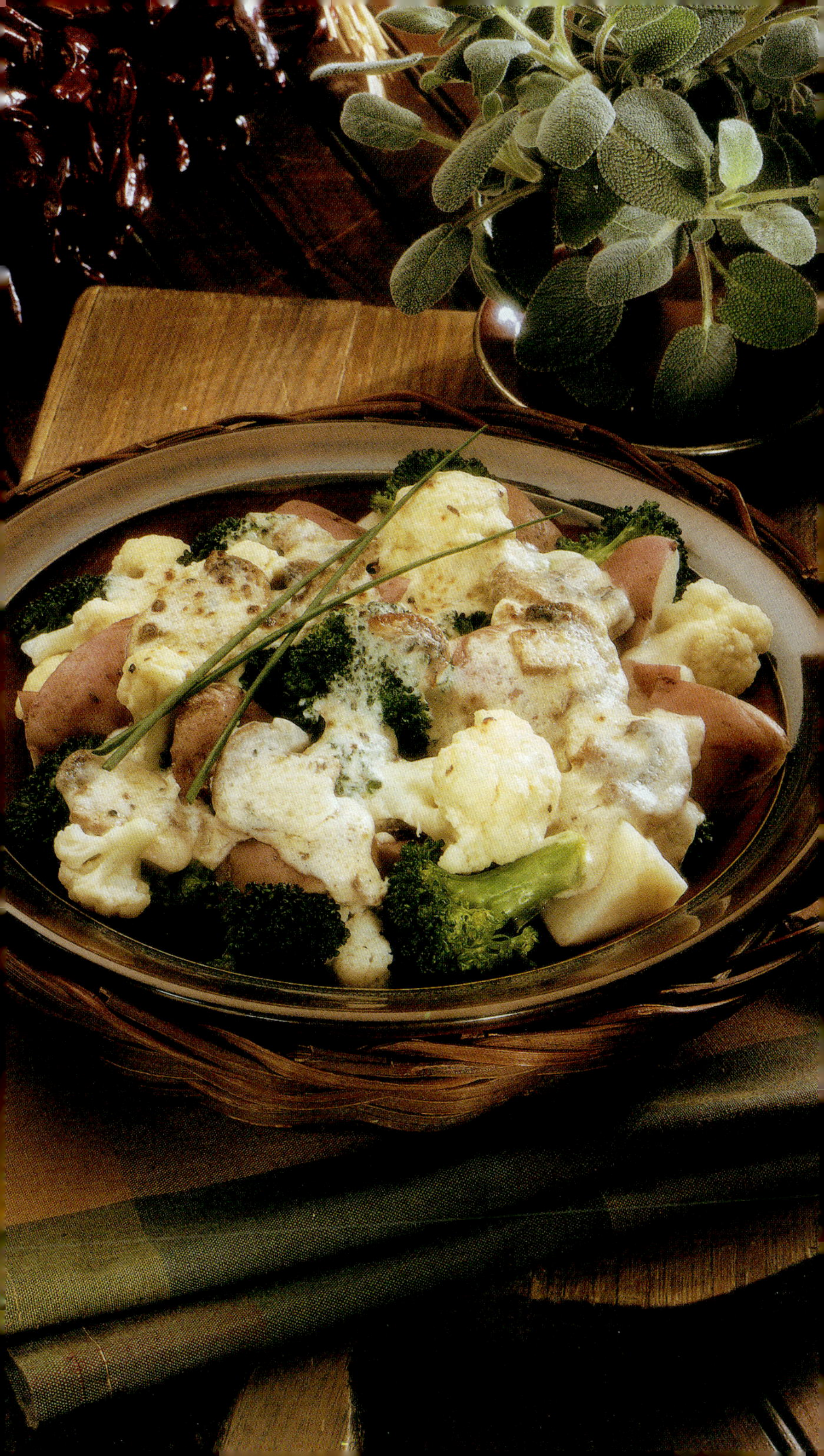

Side Dishes

Country Green Beans with Turkey-Ham

   2 teaspoons olive oil
1/4 cup minced onion
   1 clove garlic, minced
   1 pound fresh green beans, rinsed and drained
   1 cup chopped fresh tomatoes
   6 slices (2 ounces) thinly sliced low-fat smoked turkey-ham
   1 tablespoon chopped fresh marjoram
   2 teaspoons chopped fresh basil
1/8 teaspoon black pepper
1/4 cup herbed croutons

1. Heat oil in medium saucepan over medium heat. Add onion and garlic; cook and stir about 3 minutes or until onion is tender.

2. Add green beans, tomatoes, turkey-ham, marjoram, basil and pepper. Cook 10 minutes, stirring occasionally, until liquid is absorbed. Serve with croutons.   *Makes 4 servings*

✓ Honeyed Beets

1/4 cup unsweetened apple juice
   2 tablespoons cider vinegar
   1 tablespoon honey
   2 teaspoons cornstarch
   2 cans (8 ounces each) sliced beets, drained
      Salt and black pepper (optional)

Combine apple juice, vinegar, honey and cornstarch in large nonstick saucepan. Cook, stirring occasionally, over medium heat until simmering. Stir in beets and season to taste with salt and pepper, if desired. Simmer 3 minutes.   *Makes 4 servings*

Country Green Beans with Turkey-Ham

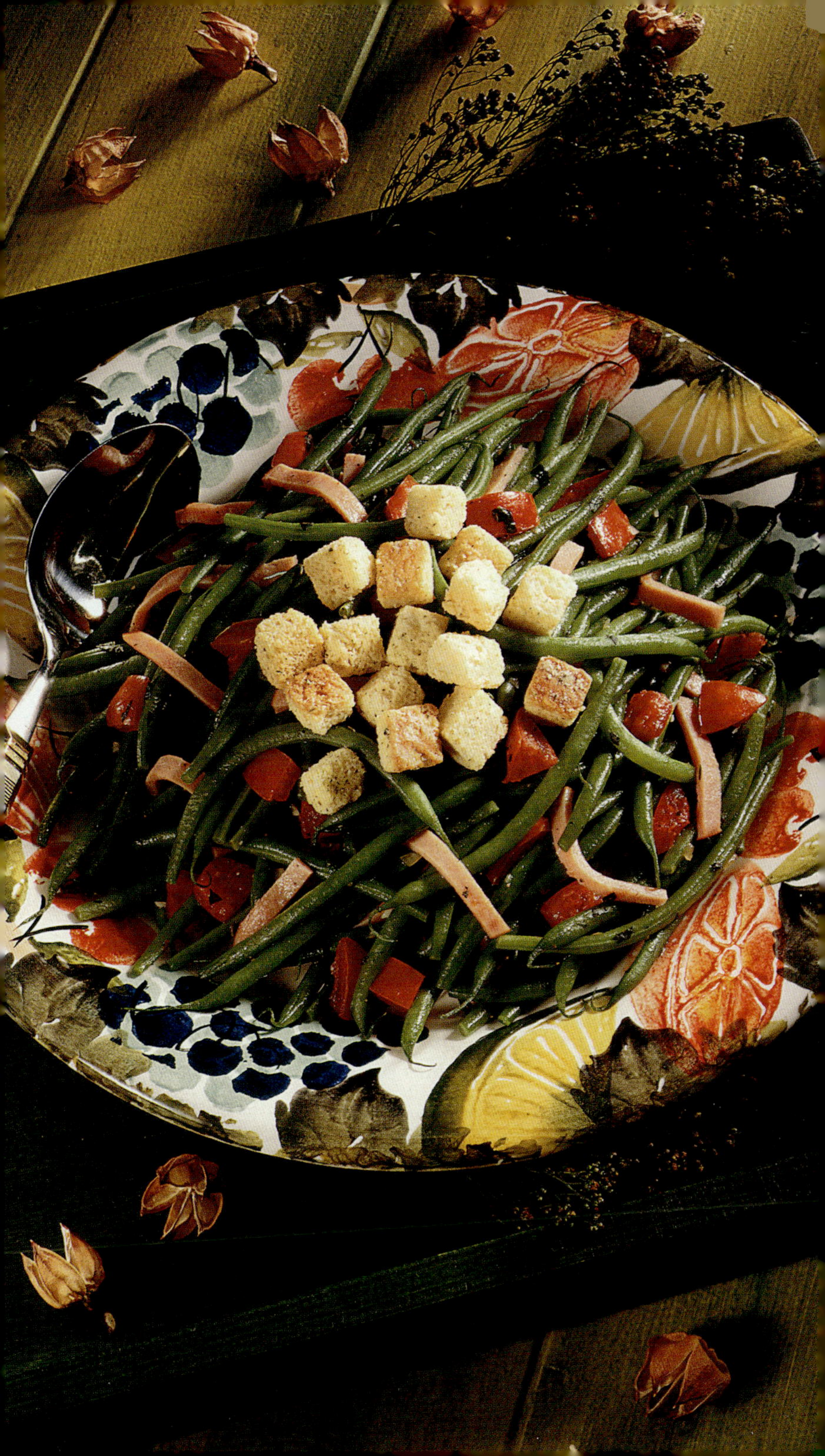

Cakes and Pies

Lemon Dream Pie

   1 prepared or homemade 9-inch pie shell
1 1/2 cups water
   1 cup honey
  1/2 cup lemon juice
  1/3 cup cornstarch
   2 tablespoons butter or margarine
   1 teaspoon grated lemon peel
  1/4 teaspoon salt
   4 egg yolks, lightly beaten
1 1/2 cups heavy whipping cream, whipped to soft peaks

Bake empty pie shell according to package directions until golden brown. In medium saucepan, combine water, honey, lemon juice, cornstarch, butter, lemon peel and salt. Bring to a boil, stirring constantly. Boil for 5 minutes. Remove from heat. Stir small amount of honey mixture into yolks. Pour yolk mixture back into honey mixture; mix thoroughly. Pour into pie shell. Chill. To serve, top with whipped cream.   Makes 8 servings

Favorite recipe from **National Honey Board**

Lemon Dream Pie

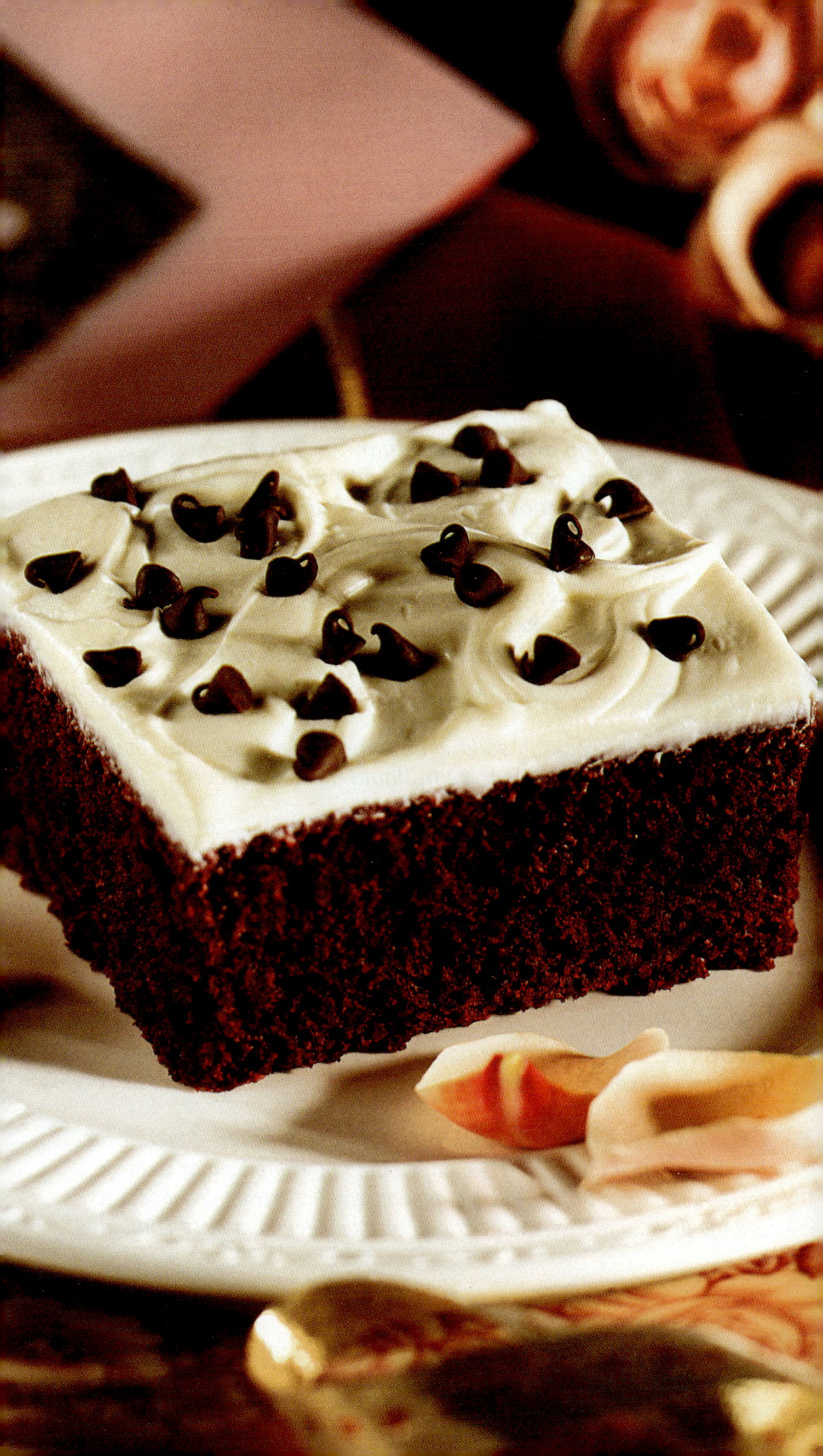

Cakes and Pies

Pumpkin Carrot Cake

  2 cups all-purpose flour
  2 teaspoons each baking soda and cinnamon
  1/2 teaspoon salt
  3/4 cup milk
  1 1/2 teaspoons lemon juice
  3 eggs
  1 1/4 cups LIBBY'S® 100% Pure Pumpkin
  1 1/2 cups granulated sugar
  1 can (8 ounces) crushed pineapple, drained
  1 cup (about 3 medium) grated carrots
  1/2 cup packed brown sugar
  1/2 cup vegetable oil
  1 1/4 cups chopped nuts, divided
  1 cup flaked coconut
  Cream Cheese Frosting (recipe follows)

PREHEAT oven to 350°F. Grease two 9-inch-round baking pans.

COMBINE flour, baking soda, cinnamon and salt in small bowl. Combine milk and lemon juice in liquid measuring cup.

BEAT eggs, pumpkin, granulated sugar, pineapple, carrots, brown sugar, oil and milk mixture in large mixer bowl; mix well. Gradually add flour mixture; beat until combined. Stir in 1 cup nuts and coconut. Pour into prepared baking pans.

BAKE for 30 to 35 minutes or until wooden pick inserted into center comes out clean. Cool in pans for 15 minutes. Remove to wire racks to cool completely.

FROST between layers, on side and top of cake with Cream Cheese Frosting. Garnish with remaining nuts.   Makes 12 servings

Cream Cheese Frosting: **COMBINE** 11 ounces softened cream cheese, 1/3 cup softened butter and 3 1/2 cups sifted powdered sugar in large mixer bowl until fluffy. Add 1 teaspoon vanilla extract, 2 teaspoons orange juice and 1 teaspoon grated orange peel; beat until combined.

Pumpkin Carrot Cake

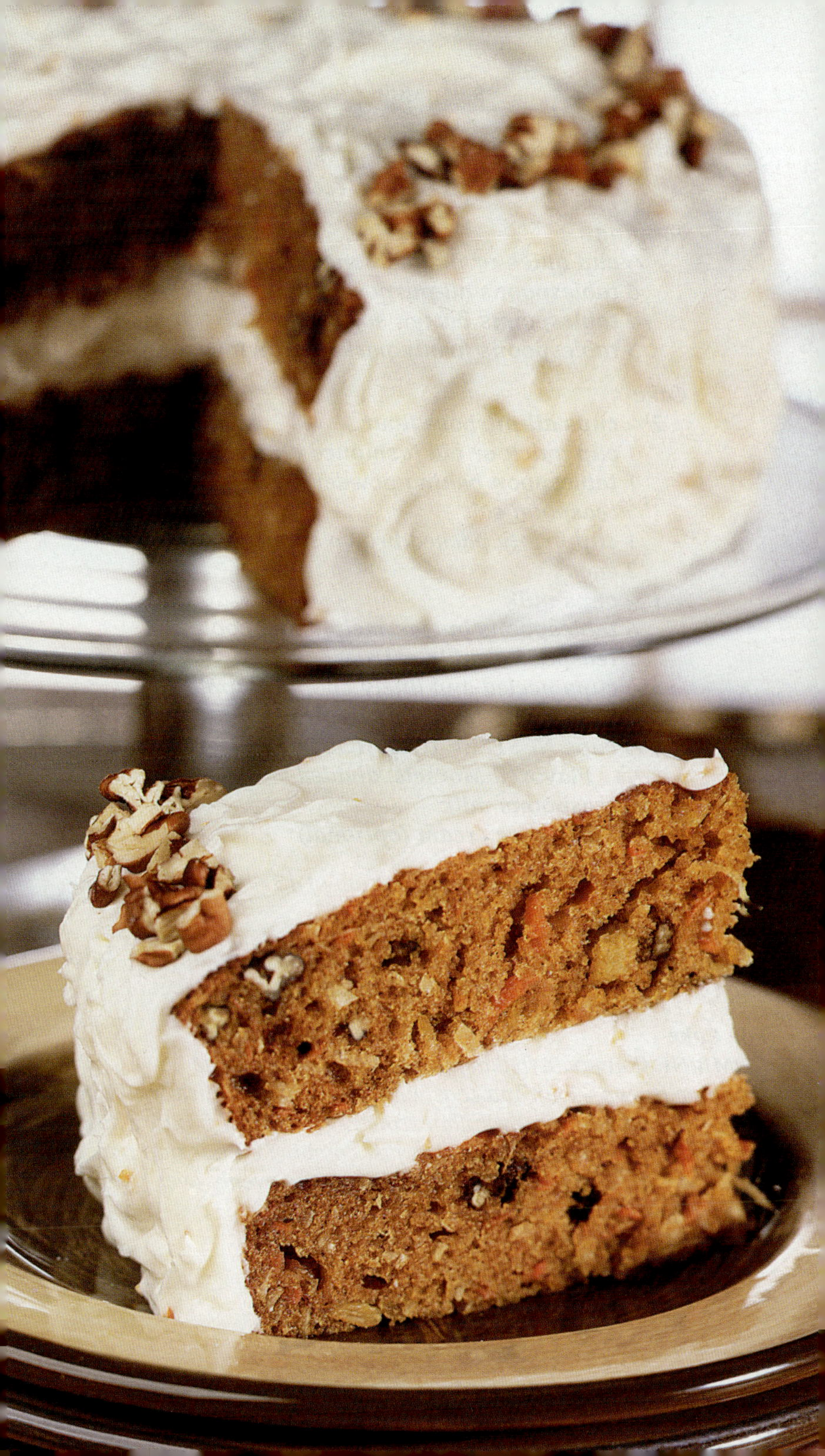

Apple-Scotch Snack Cake

Topping
- ⅔ cup quick or old fashioned oats
- 6 tablespoons all-purpose flour
- 4 tablespoons butter, softened
- 3 tablespoons firmly packed brown sugar

Cake
- 2¼ cups all-purpose flour
- 1 cup quick or old fashioned oats
- 1 tablespoon baking powder
- ½ teaspoon salt
- 1 cup firmly packed brown sugar
- 2 eggs
- 1¼ cups milk
- 6 tablespoons butter, melted and cooled
- 1 teaspoon vanilla extract
- 1⅓ cups peeled and finely chopped apple (about 2 small tart apples)
- 1⅓ cups NESTLÉ® TOLL HOUSE® Butterscotch Flavored Morsels, divided
- 1½ teaspoons milk
- Vanilla ice cream (optional)

PREHEAT oven to 350°F. Grease bottom of 13×9-inch baking pan.

For Topping
COMBINE oats, flour, butter and brown sugar in small bowl. With clean fingers, mix until crumbly; set aside.

For Cake
COMBINE flour, oats, baking powder and salt in large bowl. Combine brown sugar and eggs with wire whisk. Whisk in 1¼ cups milk, melted butter and vanilla extract. Add to flour mixture all at once; add apples. Stir gently until just combined. Pour into pan. Sprinkle with 1 cup morsels; crumble topping evenly over morsels.

Cakes and Pies

BAKE for 40 minutes or until golden brown and toothpick inserted into center comes out with a few moist crumbs clinging to it.

Remove from oven to wire rack. Microwave remaining 1/3 cup morsels and 1 1/2 teaspoons milk in small microwave-safe bowl. Microwave on HIGH (100%) power for 20 seconds; stir until smooth. Carefully drizzle over hot cake in pan. Cool in pan at least 30 minutes. Cut into squares; serve warm or at room temperature with ice cream. Store tightly covered at room temperature.

Makes 16 servings

Sour Cream Cherry Cake

1 (9-ounce) package yellow cake mix
1 egg
1 1/2 cups reduced-fat (2%) milk, divided
1 (3 1/2-ounce) package vanilla pudding mix
1/2 cup dairy sour cream
1/2 teaspoon grated lemon peel
2 cups pitted Northwest fresh sweet cherries
2 tablespoons currant jelly, melted
Mint sprigs
1 cup sweetened whipped cream (optional)

Prepare yellow cake according to package directions using egg and 1/2 cup milk. Pour batter into flan pan and bake according to package directions. Prepare vanilla pudding according to package directions using 1 cup milk; remove from heat and stir in sour cream and lemon peel. When cake is cool, top with vanilla pudding. Top with cherries; brush with melted jelly. Garnish with mint. Serve with whipped cream, if desired.

Makes 8 servings

Favorite recipe from **Northwest Cherry Growers**

Desserts

Chilled Cherry Cheesecake

4 chocolate graham crackers, crushed
(1 cup crumbs)
12 ounces Neufchâtel cheese
8 ounces vanilla fat-free yogurt
¼ cup sugar
1 teaspoon vanilla
1 envelope unflavored gelatin
¼ cup cold water
1 can (20 ounces) light cherry pie filling

1. Sprinkle cracker crumbs on bottom of 8-inch square baking pan. Beat cheese, yogurt, sugar and vanilla in medium bowl with electric mixer until smooth and creamy.

2. Sprinkle gelatin into water in small microwavable cup; let stand 2 minutes. Microwave at HIGH 40 seconds, stir and let stand 2 minutes or until gelatin is completely dissolved.

3. Gradually beat gelatin mixture into cheese mixture with electric mixer until well blended. Pour into prepared pan; refrigerate until firm. Spoon cherry topping onto cheesecake. Refrigerate until ready to serve. *Makes 9 servings*

Chilled Cherry Cheesecake

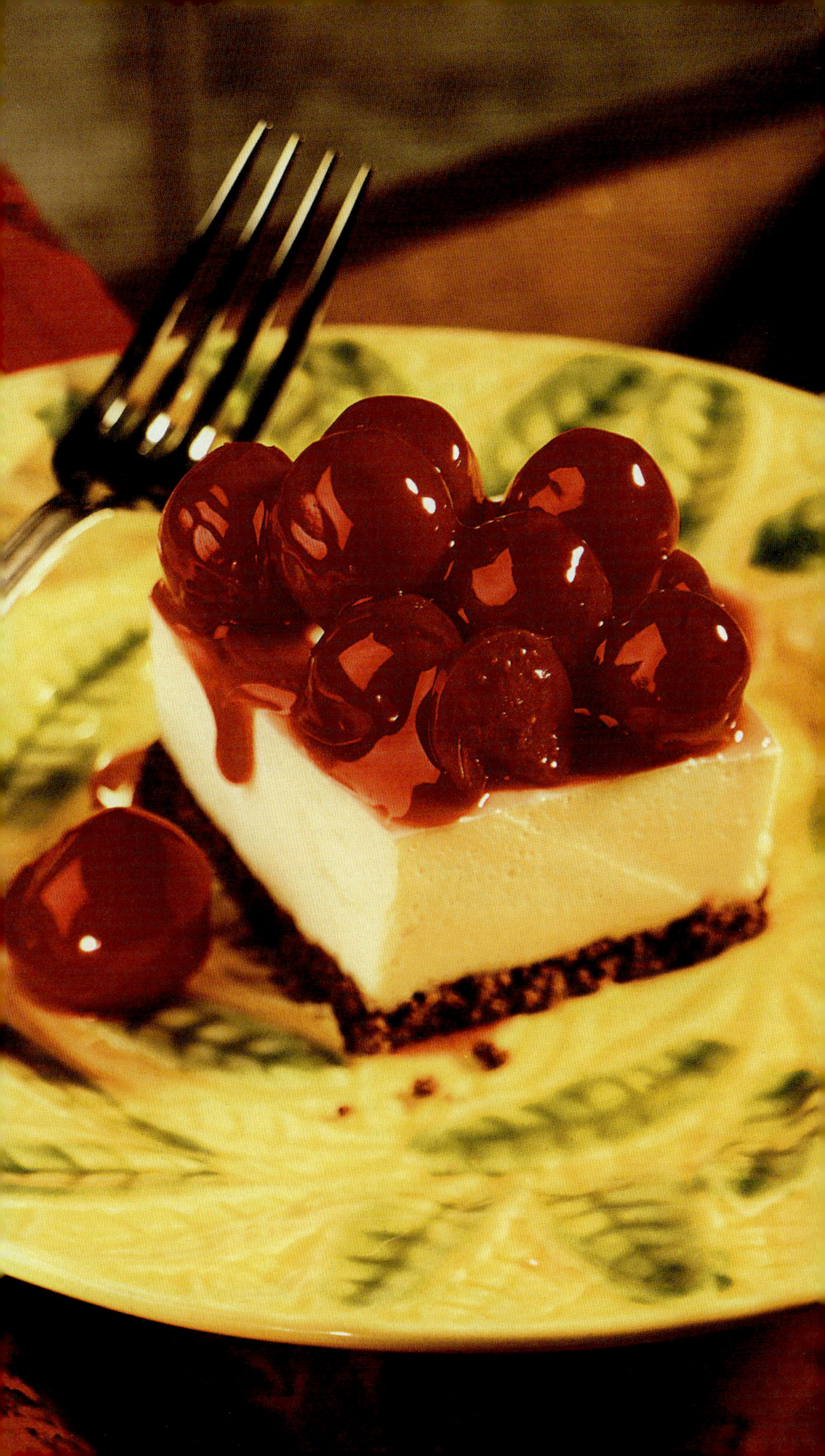

Desserts

Toffee Bread Pudding with Cinnamon Toffee Sauce

3 cups milk
4 eggs
3/4 cup sugar
3/4 teaspoon ground cinnamon
3/4 teaspoon vanilla extract
1/2 teaspoon salt
6 to 6 1/2 cups 1/2-inch cubes French, Italian or sourdough bread
1 cup SKOR® English Toffee Bits or HEATH® BITS 'O BRICKLE® Almond Toffee Bits, divided
Cinnamon Toffee Sauce (recipe follows)
Sweetened whipped cream or ice cream (optional)

1. Heat oven to 350°F. Butter 13×9×2-inch baking pan.

2. Mix together milk, eggs, sugar, cinnamon, vanilla and salt in large bowl with wire whisk. Stir in bread cubes, coating completely. Allow to stand 10 minutes. Stir in 1/2 cup toffee bits. Pour into prepared pan. Sprinkle remaining 1/2 cup toffee bits over surface.

3. Bake 40 to 45 minutes or until surface is set. Cool 30 minutes.

4. Meanwhile, prepare Cinnamon Toffee Sauce. Cut pudding into squares; top with sauce and sweetened whipped cream or ice cream, if desired.   Makes 12 servings

Cinnamon Toffee Sauce: Combine 3/4 cup SKOR® English Toffee Bits or HEATH® BITS 'O BRICKLE® Almond Toffee Bits, 1/3 cup whipping cream and 1/8 teaspoon ground cinnamon in medium saucepan. Cook over low heat, stirring constantly, until toffee melts and mixture is well blended. (As toffee melts, small bits of almond will remain.) Makes about 2/3 cup sauce.

Note: This dessert is best eaten the same day it is prepared.

Toffee Bread Pudding with Cinnamon Toffee Sauce

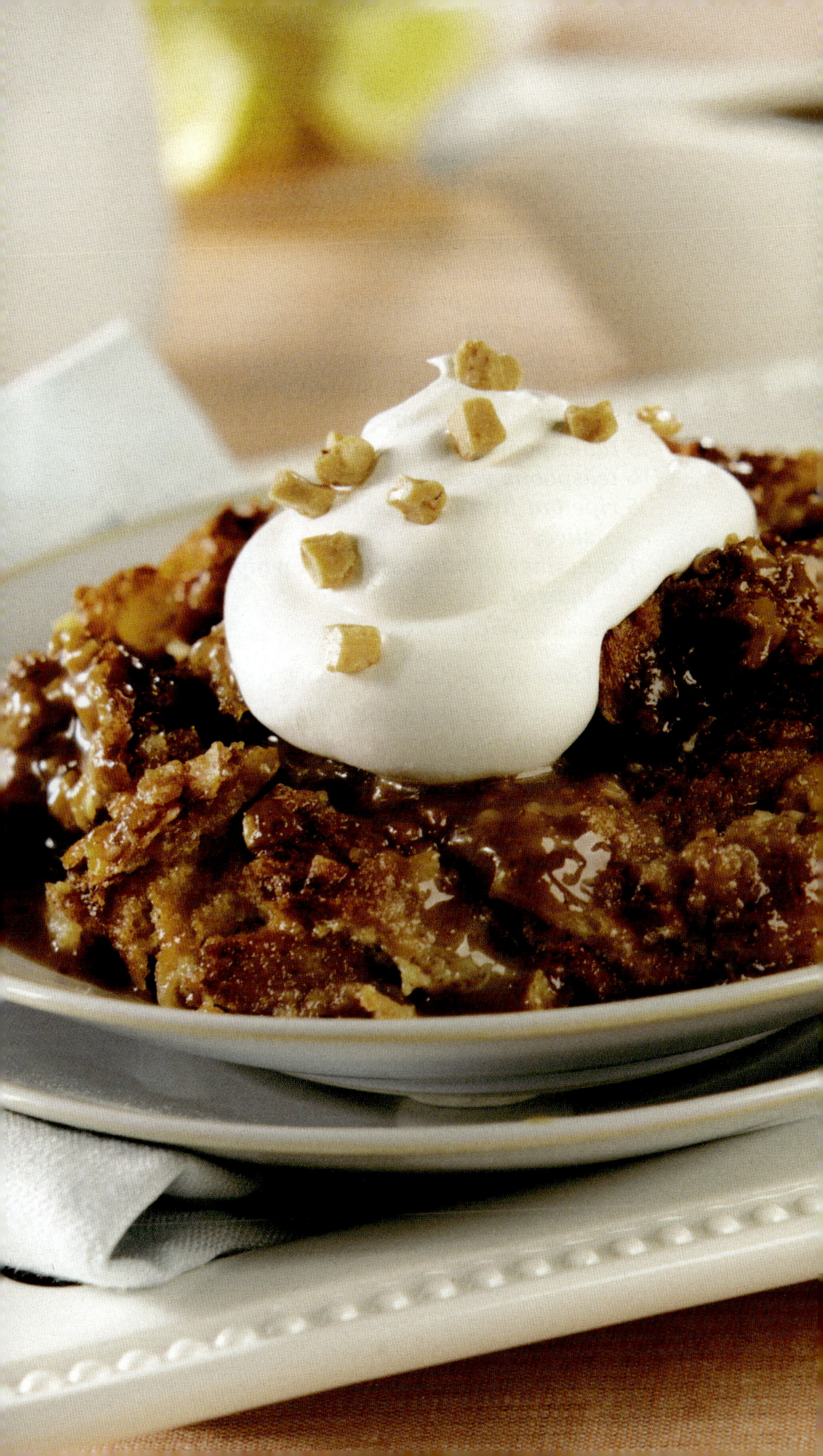

Desserts

Banana Pudding

60 to 70 vanilla wafers*
1 cup granulated sugar
3 tablespoons cornstarch
1/4 teaspoon salt
2 cans (12 fluid ounces each) NESTLÉ® CARNATION® Evaporated Milk
2 eggs, lightly beaten
3 tablespoons butter, cut into pieces
1 1/2 teaspoons vanilla extract
5 ripe but firm large bananas, cut into 1/4-inch slices
1 container (8 ounces) frozen whipped topping, thawed

*A 12-ounce box of vanilla wafers contains about 88 wafers.

LINE bottom and side of 2 1/2-quart glass bowl with about 40 wafers.

COMBINE sugar, cornstarch and salt in medium saucepan. Gradually stir in evaporated milk to dissolve cornstarch. Whisk in eggs. Add butter. Cook over medium heat, stirring constantly, until the mixture begins to thicken. Reduce heat to low; simmer 1 minute, stirring constantly. Remove from heat. Stir in vanilla extract. Let cool slightly.

POUR half of pudding over wafers. Top with half of bananas. Layer remaining vanilla wafers over bananas. Combine remaining pudding and bananas; spoon over wafers. Refrigerate for at least 4 hours. Top with whipped topping.

Makes 8 servings

Desserts

Baked Apples

2 tablespoons sugar
2 tablespoons raisins, chopped
2 tablespoons chopped walnuts
2 tablespoons GRANDMA'S® Molasses
6 apples, cored

Heat oven to 350°F. In medium bowl, combine sugar, raisins, walnuts and molasses. Fill apple cavities with molasses mixture. Place in 13×9-inch baking dish. Pour 1/2 cup hot water over apples and bake 25 minutes or until soft.   *Makes 6 servings*

Winter Fruit Compote

1 can (16 ounces) pitted dark sweet cherries in syrup, undrained
1 teaspoon cornstarch
1 tablespoon almond-flavored liqueur (amaretto) or 1/2 teaspoon almond extract
1 1/2 tablespoons honey
2 ripe Bartlett or Comice pears, peeled, cored and cut into 1-inch cubes
1 teaspoon chopped fresh mint
Mint sprigs (optional)

1. *Drain cherries reserving 1/4 cup liquid. Combine reserved liquid and cornstarch in small bowl; mix until smooth. Add mixture to saucepan and bring to boil, over medium-high heat; stirring frequently. Reduce heat to simmer, as mixture begins to thicken, stir in liqueur and honey.*

2. *Stir in pears and drained cherries. Cook 2 minutes or until fruit is warm, stirring occasionally. Spoon into dessert dishes; sprinkle with mint and garnish with mint sprigs, if desired. Serve warm or at room temperature.*   *Makes 4 servings*

Desserts

Lemon Cheesecake

Crust
- 35 vanilla wafers
- 3/4 cup slivered almonds, toasted
- 1/3 cup sugar
- 1/4 cup butter, melted

Filling
- 3 packages (8 ounces each) cream cheese, softened
- 3/4 cup sugar
- 4 eggs
- 1/3 cup whipping cream
- 1 tablespoon grated lemon peel
- 1/4 cup lemon juice
- 1 teaspoon vanilla

Topping
- 1 pint strawberries
- 2 tablespoons sugar

1. Preheat oven to 375°F. For crust, combine wafers, almonds and 1/3 cup sugar in food processor; process until fine crumbs are formed. Combine crumb mixture with melted butter in medium bowl. Press mixture evenly on bottom and 1 inch up side of 9-inch springform pan. Set aside.

2. For filling, beat cream cheese and 3/4 cup sugar in large bowl at high speed of electric mixer 2 to 3 minutes or until fluffy. Add eggs one at a time, beating after each addition. Add whipping cream, lemon peel, lemon juice and vanilla; beat just until blended. Pour into prepared crust. Place springform pan on baking sheet. Bake 45 to 55 minutes or until set. Run spatula around edge of cheesecake to loosen from pan. Cool completely on wire rack. Cover and refrigerate at least 10 hours or overnight.

3. To complete recipe, for topping, hull and slice strawberries. Combine with 2 tablespoons sugar in medium bowl. Let stand 15 minutes. Serve over cheesecake.   *Makes 16 servings*

Lemon Cheesecake

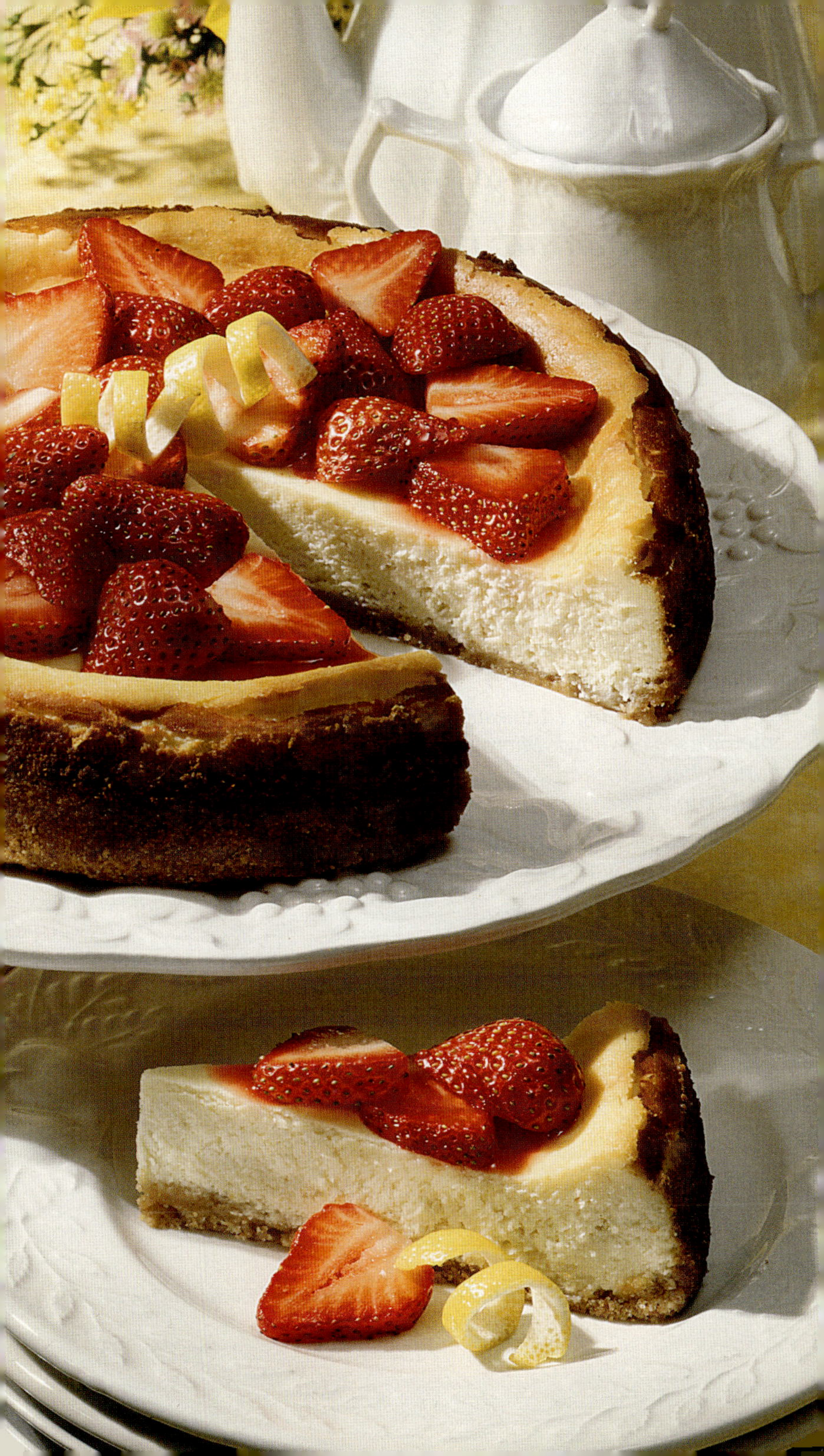

Desserts

Baked Apple Slices with Peanut Butter Crumble

4 cups peeled and thinly sliced apples
1 cup sugar, divided
1 cup all-purpose flour, divided
3 tablespoons butter or margarine, divided
1 cup quick-cooking or old-fashioned rolled oats
1/2 teaspoon ground cinnamon
1 cup REESE'S® Creamy or Crunchy Peanut Butter
Sweetened whipped cream or ice cream (optional)

1. Heat oven to 350°F. Grease 9-inch square baking pan.

2. Stir together apples, 3/4 cup sugar and 1/4 cup flour in large bowl. Spread in prepared pan; dot with 2 tablespoons butter. Combine oats, remaining 3/4 cup flour, remaining 1/4 cup sugar and cinnamon in medium bowl; set aside.

3. Place remaining 1 tablespoon butter and peanut butter in small microwave-safe bowl. Microwave at HIGH (100%) 30 seconds or until butter is melted; stir until smooth. Add to oat mixture; blend until crumbs are formed. Sprinkle crumb mixture over apples.

4. Bake 40 to 45 minutes or until apples are tender and edges are bubbly. Cool slightly. Serve warm or cool with whipped cream or ice cream, if desired.

Makes 6 to 8 servings

Baked Apple Slices with Peanut Butter Crumble

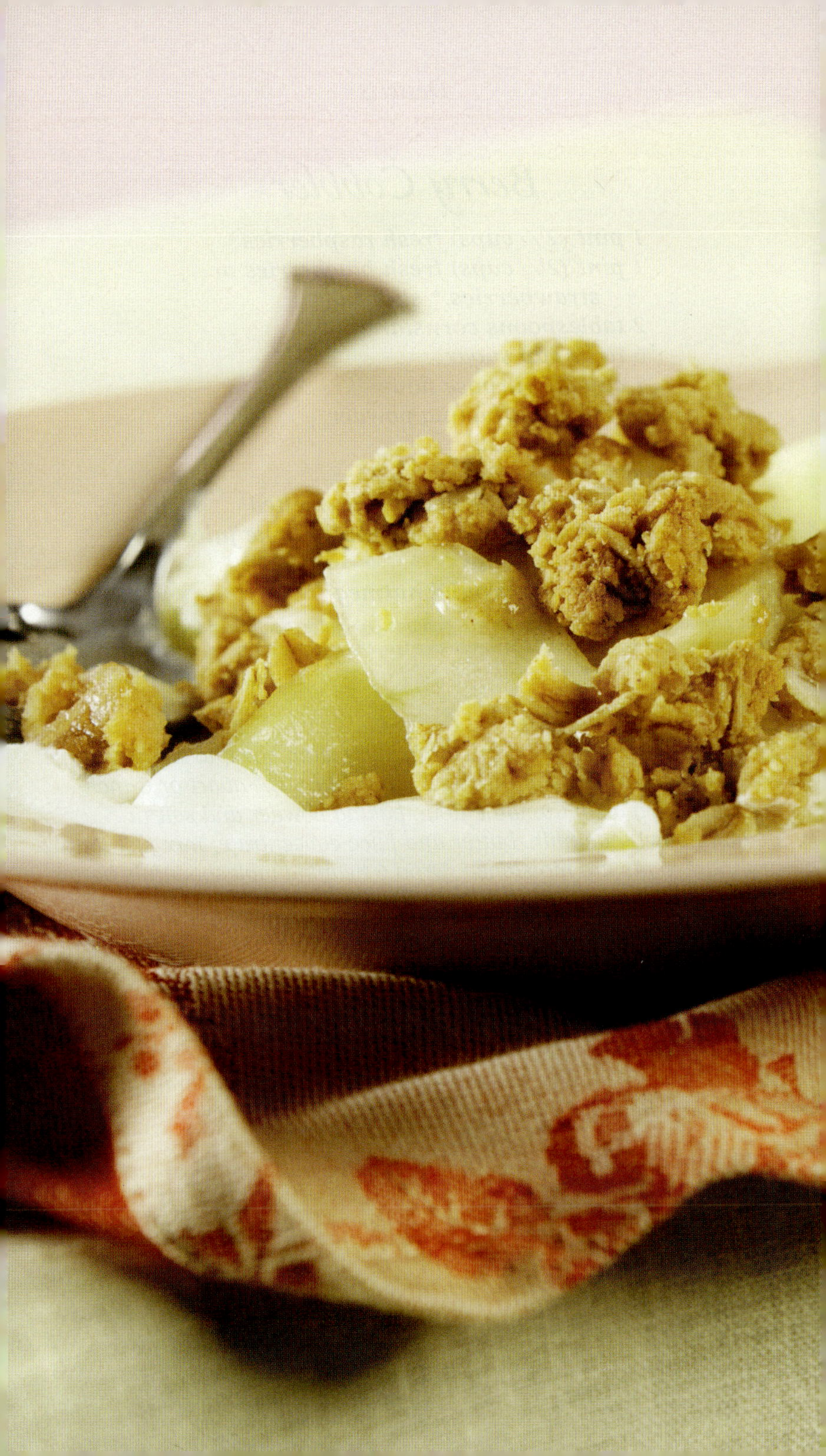

Desserts

Berry Cobbler

1 pint (2½ cups) fresh raspberries*
1 pint (2½ cups) fresh blueberries or strawberries,* sliced
2 tablespoons cornstarch
½ to ¾ cup sugar
1 cup all-purpose flour
1½ teaspoons baking powder
¼ teaspoon salt
⅓ cup milk
⅓ cup butter or margarine, melted
2 tablespoons thawed frozen apple juice concentrate
¼ teaspoon ground nutmeg

*One (16-ounce) bag frozen raspberries and one (16-ounce) bag frozen blueberries or strawberries can be substituted for fresh berries. Thaw berries, reserving juices. Increase cornstarch to 3 tablespoons.

1. Preheat oven to 375°F.

2. Combine berries and cornstarch in medium bowl; toss lightly to coat. Add sugar to taste; mix well. Spoon into 1½-quart or 8-inch square baking dish. Combine flour, baking powder and salt in medium bowl. Add milk, butter and juice concentrate; mix just until dry ingredients are moistened. Drop 6 heaping tablespoonfuls batter evenly over berries; sprinkle with nutmeg.

3. Bake 25 minutes or until topping is golden brown and fruit is bubbly. Cool on wire rack. Serve warm or at room temperature.

Makes 6 servings

Tip: Cobblers are best served warm or at room temperature on the day they are made. Leftovers should be kept covered and refrigerated for up to two days. Reheat them, covered, at 350°F until warm.

Prep Time: 5 minutes
Bake Time: 25 minutes

Desserts

Classic Rice Pudding

1 (14-ounce) can EAGLE BRAND® Sweetened Condensed Milk (NOT evaporated milk)
2 egg yolks
1/4 cup water
1/2 teaspoon ground cinnamon
2 cups uncooked long grain rice, cooked
1/2 cup raisins
2 teaspoons vanilla extract
Additional ground cinnamon

1. In large saucepan, combine EAGLE BRAND®, egg yolks, water and cinnamon. Over medium heat, cook and stir 10 to 15 minutes or until mixture thickens slightly.

2. Remove from heat; add cooked rice, raisins and vanilla. Cool. Chill thoroughly. Sprinkle with additional cinnamon. Refrigerate leftovers. *Makes 8 to 10 servings*

Ambrosia

1 can (20 ounces) DOLE® Pineapple Chunks, drained
1 can (11 or 15 ounces) DOLE® Mandarin Oranges, drained
1 DOLE® Banana, sliced
1 1/2 cups seedless grapes
1/2 cup miniature marshmallows
1 cup vanilla lowfat yogurt
1/4 cup flaked coconut, toasted

- Combine pineapple chunks, mandarin oranges, banana, grapes and marshmallows in medium bowl.
- Stir yogurt into fruit mixture. Sprinkle with coconut.

Makes 4 to 6 servings

Prep Time: 15 minutes

Cookies and Brownies

Layered Cookie Bars

3/4 cup (1 1/2 sticks) butter or margarine
1 3/4 cups vanilla wafer crumbs
6 tablespoons HERSHEY'S Cocoa
1/4 cup sugar
1 can (14 ounces) sweetened condensed milk
1 cup HERSHEY'S Semi-Sweet Chocolate Chips
3/4 cup SKOR® English Toffee Bits
1 cup chopped walnuts

1. Heat oven to 350°F. Melt butter in 13×9×2-inch baking pan in oven. Combine crumbs, cocoa and sugar; sprinkle over butter.

2. Pour sweetened condensed milk evenly on top of crumbs. Top with chocolate chips and toffee bits, then nuts; press down firmly.

3. Bake 25 to 30 minutes or until lightly browned. Cool completely in pan on wire rack. Chill, if desired. Cut into bars. Store covered at room temperature.

Makes about 36 bars

Layered Cookie Bars

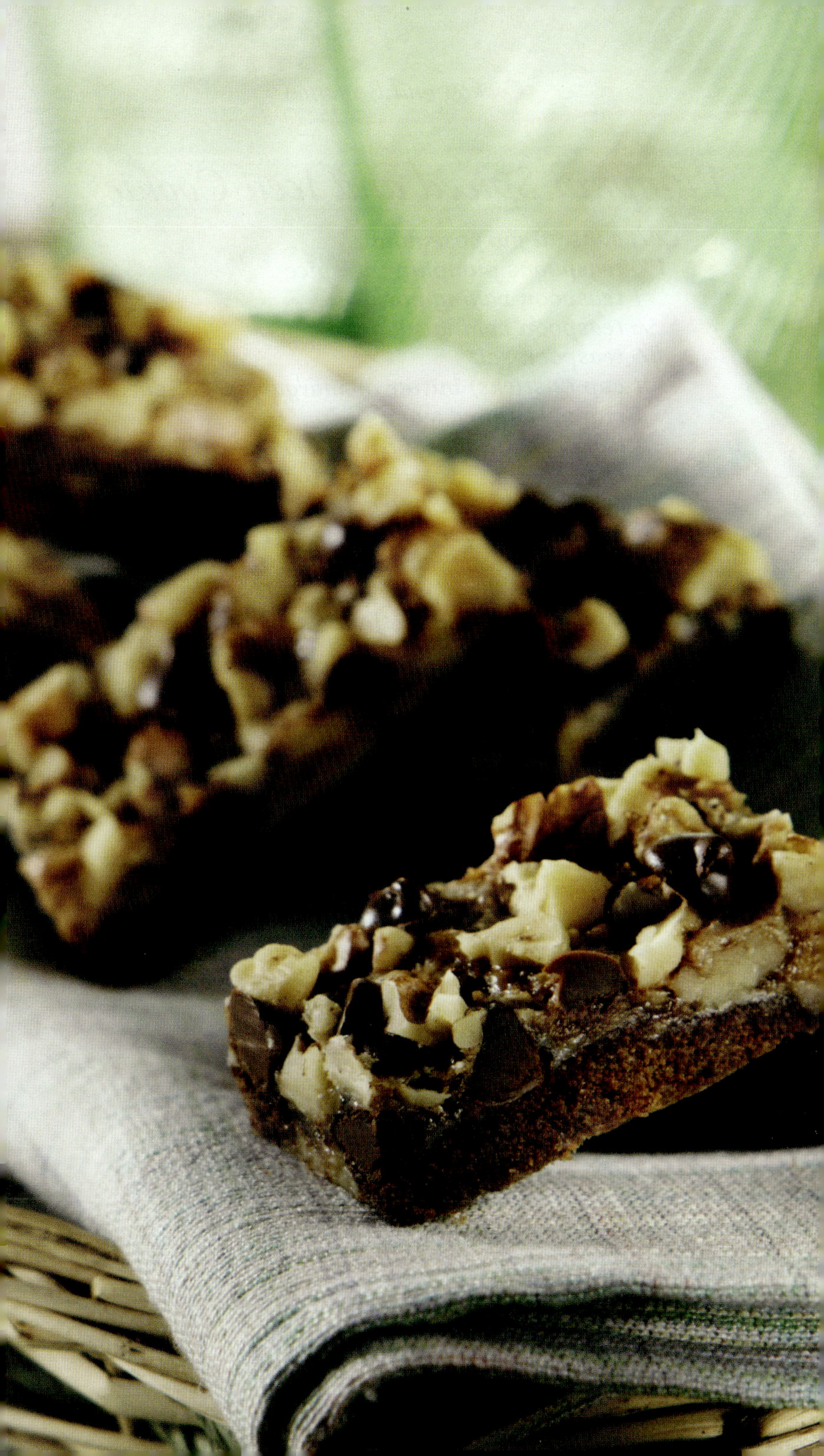

Cookies and Brownies

Pumpkin Spiced and Iced Cookies

2¼ cups all-purpose flour
1½ teaspoons pumpkin pie spice
1 teaspoon baking powder
½ teaspoon baking soda
½ teaspoon salt
1 cup (2 sticks) butter or margarine, softened
1 cup granulated sugar
1 can (15 ounces) LIBBY'S® 100% Pure Pumpkin
2 eggs
1 teaspoon vanilla extract
2 cups (12-ounce package) NESTLÉ® TOLL HOUSE® Semi-Sweet Chocolate Morsels
1 cup chopped walnuts (optional)
Vanilla Glaze (recipe follows)

PREHEAT oven to 375°F. Grease baking sheets.

COMBINE flour, pumpkin pie spice, baking powder, baking soda and salt in medium bowl. Beat butter and granulated sugar in large mixer bowl until creamy. Beat in pumpkin, eggs and vanilla extract. Gradually beat in flour mixture. Stir in morsels and nuts. Drop by rounded tablespoon onto prepared baking sheets.

BAKE for 15 to 20 minutes or until edges are lightly browned. Cool on baking sheets for 2 minutes; remove to wire rack to cool completely. Spread or drizzle with Vanilla Glaze.

Makes about 5½ dozen cookies

Vanilla Glaze: **COMBINE** 1 cup powdered sugar, 1 to 1½ tablespoons milk and ½ teaspoon vanilla extract in small bowl; mix well.

Pumpkin Spiced and Iced Cookies

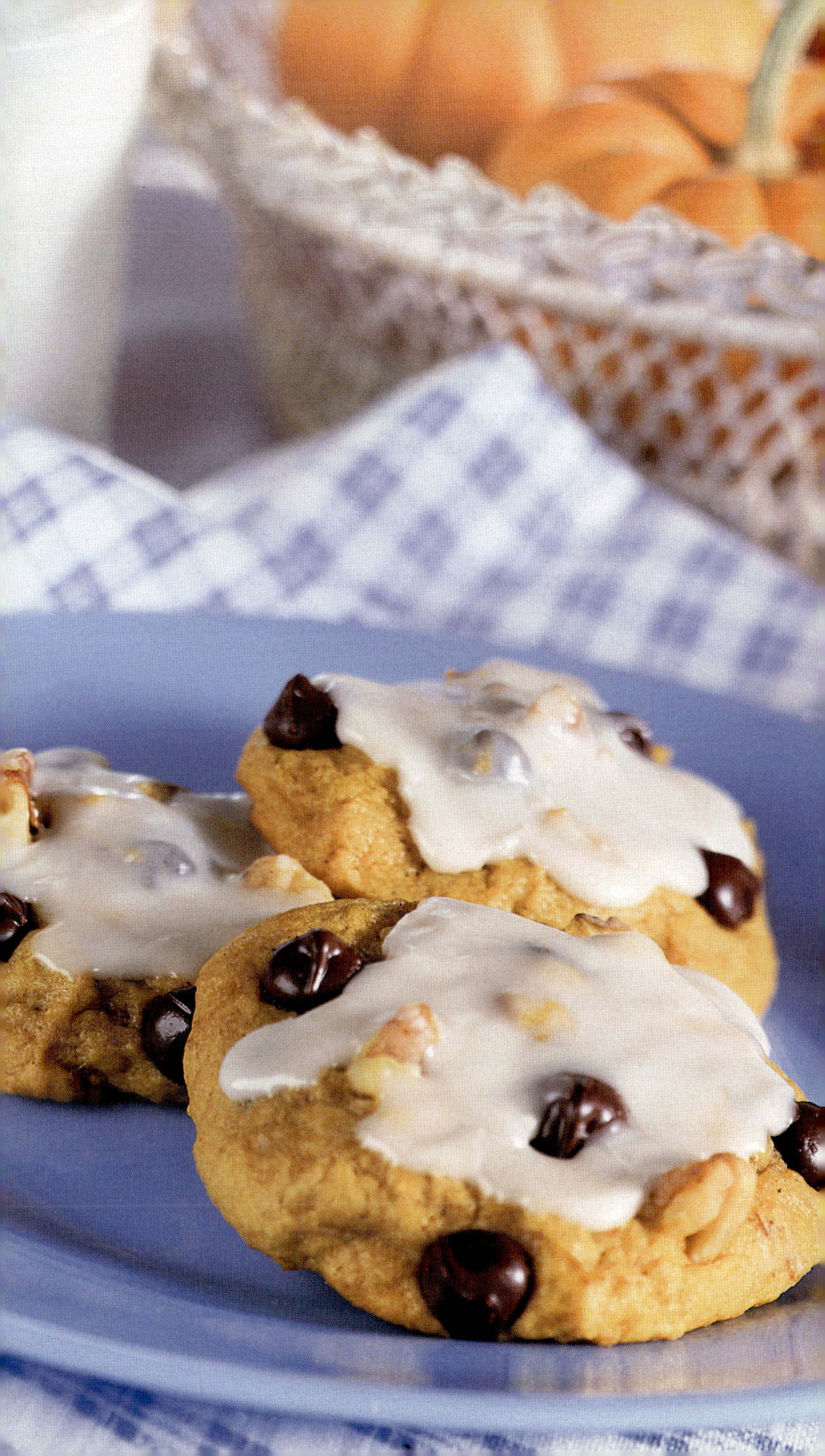

Cookies & Brownies

Chocolate Peanut Butter Shortbread Bars

Chocolate Shortbread
 1 cup butter, softened
 3/4 cup sugar
 1/3 cup unsweetened cocoa
 1 teaspoon vanilla extract
 2 cups all-purpose flour

Peanut Butter Layer
 1 cup butter, softened
 1 cup sugar
 1/4 cup crunchy peanut butter
 1 egg yolk
 1 teaspoon vanilla extract
 1 1/3 cups all-purpose flour
 1 cup rolled oats
 1/2 cup dry-roasted peanuts, finely chopped

Preheat oven to 300°F.

To make chocolate shortbread: In a bowl, cream together the butter, sugar, cocoa and vanilla. Mix in the flour until smooth. Set aside.

To make peanut butter layer: Cream together the butter, sugar and peanut butter. Add the egg yolk and vanilla. Mix in flour and oats.

Grease a 13×9-inch baking dish. Pat half of the chocolate shortbread into the pan. (This will be a thin layer.) Spread the peanut butter layer over the chocolate layer. Carefully pat the remaining shortbread dough evenly over the peanut butter layer to cover completely. Gently pat peanuts into the shortbread.

Bake for about 1 hour, checking after 45 minutes. The shortbread will be done when the sides look dry. Cut into squares while still hot. Let the shortbread cool before removing from the pan.

Makes 32 bars

Favorite recipe from **Texas Peanut Producers Board**

Chocolate Peanut Butter Shortbread Bars

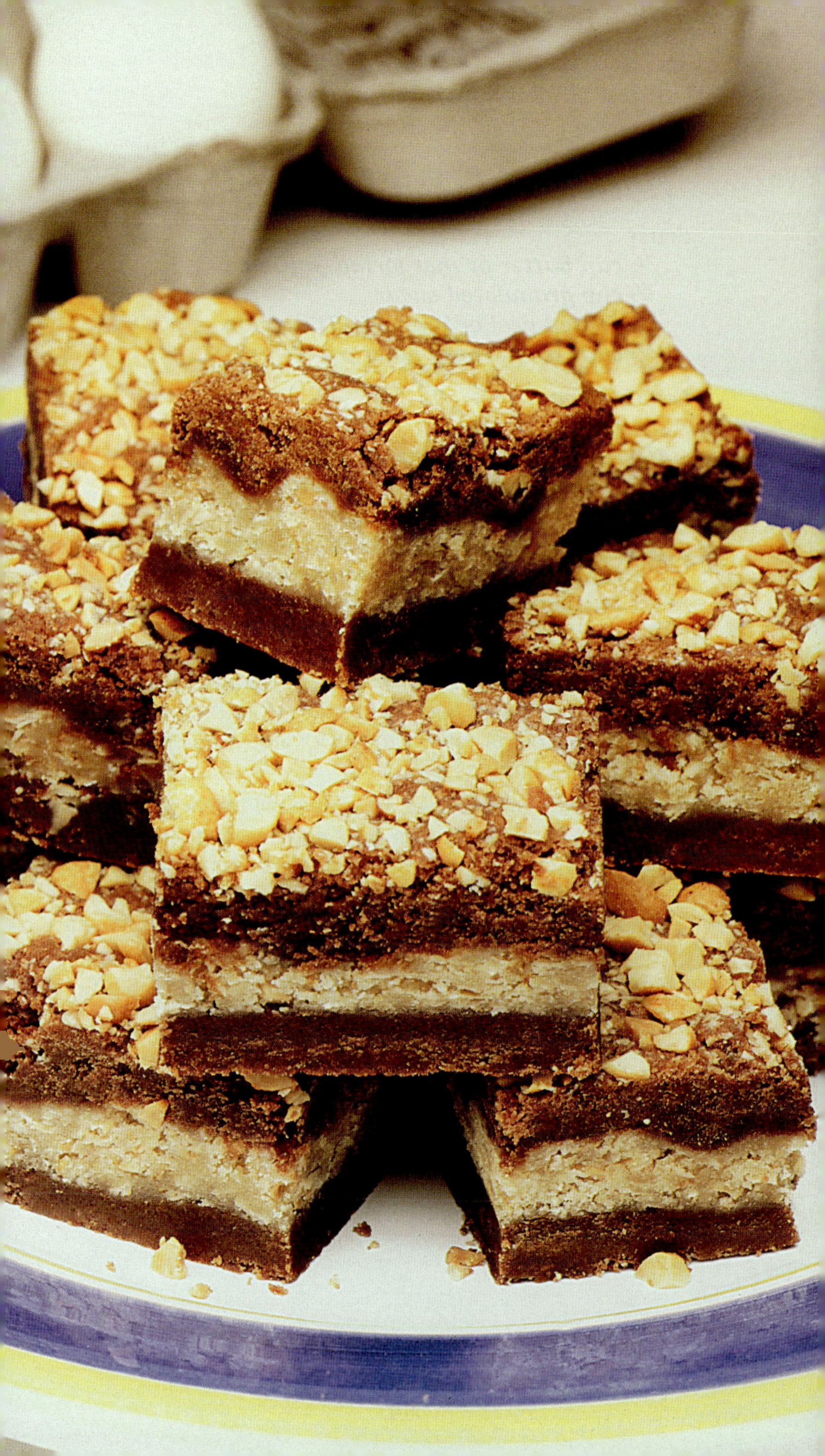

Cookies & Brownies

Luscious Fresh Lemon Bars

Crust
- 1/2 cup butter or margarine, softened
- 1/2 cup granulated sugar
- Grated peel of 1/2 SUNKIST® lemon
- 1 1/4 cups all-purpose flour

Lemon Layer
- 4 eggs
- 1 2/3 cups granulated sugar
- 3 tablespoons all-purpose flour
- 1/2 teaspoon baking powder
- Grated peel of 1/2 SUNKIST® lemon
- Juice of 2 SUNKIST® lemons (6 tablespoons)
- 1 teaspoon vanilla extract
- Confectioners' sugar

To make crust, in bowl blend together butter, granulated sugar and lemon peel. Gradually stir in flour to form a soft crumbly dough. Press evenly into bottom of foil-lined 13×9×2-inch baking pan. Bake at 350°F for 15 minutes.

Meanwhile, to prepare lemon layer, in large bowl whisk or beat eggs well. Stir together granulated sugar, flour and baking powder. Gradually whisk sugar mixture into beaten eggs. Stir or whisk in lemon peel, lemon juice and vanilla. Pour over hot baked crust. Return to oven and bake for 20 to 25 minutes, or until top and sides are lightly browned. Cool. Using foil on two sides, lift out the cookie base and gently loosen foil along all sides. With a long wet knife, cut into bars or squares. Sprinkle tops with confectioners' sugar.

Makes about 3 dozen bars

Cookies & Brownies

Dad's Ginger Molasses Cookies

> 1 cup granulated sugar
> 1 cup shortening
> 1 tablespoon baking soda
> 2 teaspoons ground ginger
> 2 teaspoons ground cinnamon
> 1 teaspoon ground cloves
> 1/2 teaspoon salt
> 1 cup molasses
> 2/3 cup double-strength instant coffee*
> 1 egg
> 4 3/4 cups all-purpose flour

*To prepare double-strength coffee, follow instructions for instant coffee but use twice the recommended amount of instant coffee granules.

1. Preheat oven to 350°F. Lightly grease cookie sheets.

2. Beat sugar and shortening with electric mixer until creamy. Beat in baking soda, ginger, cinnamon, cloves and salt until well blended. Add molasses, coffee and egg, one at a time, beating well after each addition. Gradually add flour, beating on low speed just until blended.

3. Drop dough by rounded tablespoonfuls 2 inches apart on prepared cookie sheets. Bake 12 to 15 minutes or until cookies are set but not browned. Cool on cookie sheets 1 minute. Remove to wire racks; cool completely.

Makes about 6 dozen cookies

Cookies & Brownies

Rocky Road Brownies

1 cup miniature marshmallows
1¼ cups HERSHEY®S Semi-Sweet Chocolate Chips
½ cup chopped nuts
½ cup (1 stick) butter or margarine
1 cup sugar
2 eggs
1 teaspoon vanilla extract
½ cup all-purpose flour
⅓ cup HERSHEY®S Cocoa
½ teaspoon baking powder
½ teaspoon salt

1. Heat oven to 350°F. Grease 9-inch square baking pan.

2. Stir together marshmallows, chocolate chips and nuts; set aside. Place butter in large microwave-safe bowl. Microwave at HIGH (100% power) 1 to 1½ minutes or until melted. Add sugar, eggs and vanilla, beating with spoon until well blended. Add flour, cocoa, baking powder and salt; blend well. Spread batter in prepared pan.

3. Bake 22 minutes. Sprinkle chocolate chip mixture over top. Continue baking 5 minutes or until marshmallows have softened and puffed slightly. Cool completely. With wet knife, cut into squares.

Makes about 20 brownies

Rocky Road Brownies

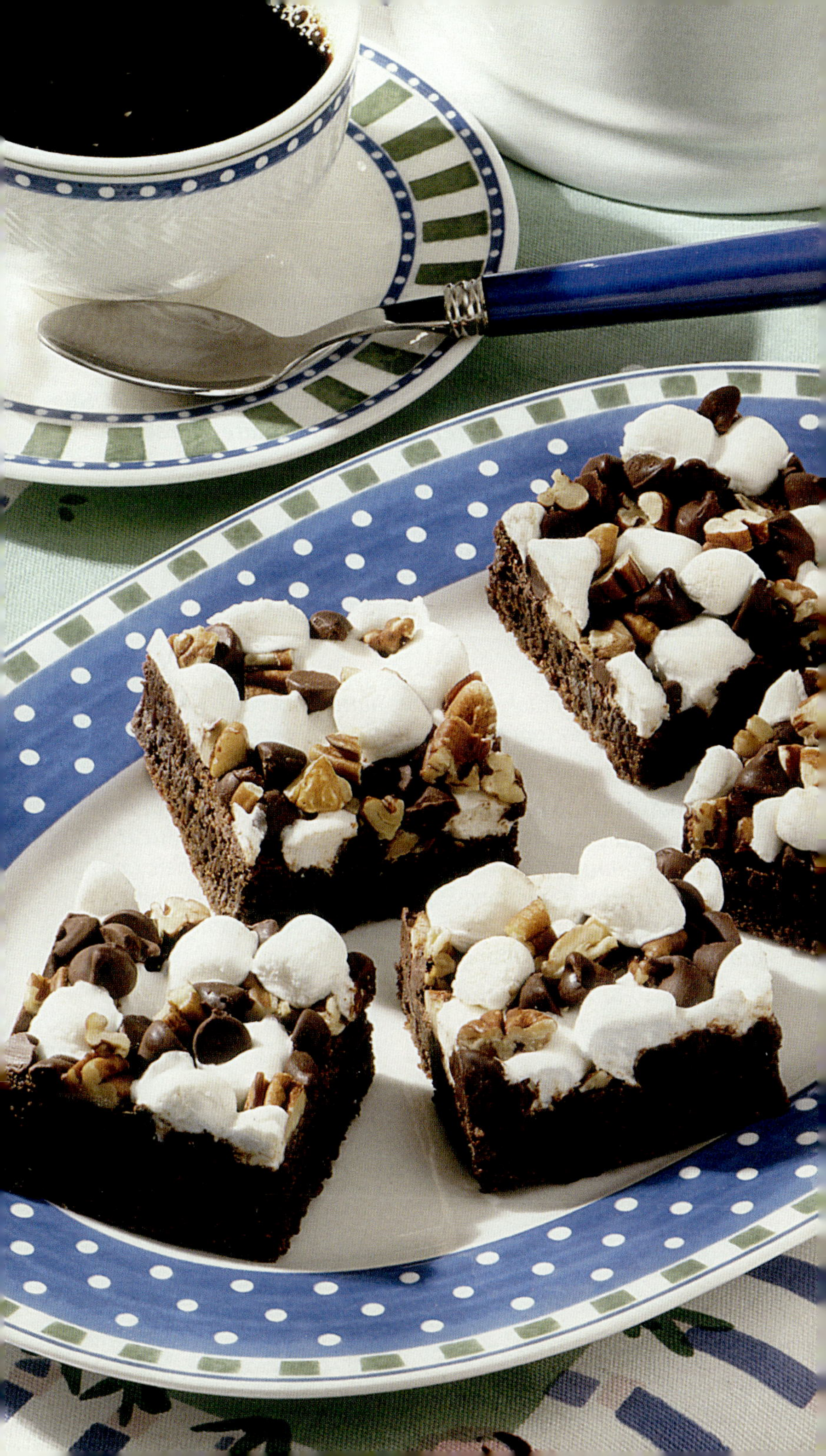

Peanutty Gooey Bars

Crust
- 2 cups chocolate graham cracker crumbs
- 1/2 cup (1 stick) butter or margarine, melted
- 1/3 cup granulated sugar

Topping
- 1 2/3 cups (11-ounce package) NESTLÉ® TOLL HOUSE® Peanut Butter & Milk Chocolate Morsels, divided
- 1 can (14 ounces) NESTLÉ® CARNATION® Sweetened Condensed Milk
- 1 teaspoon vanilla extract
- 1 cup coarsely chopped peanuts

PREHEAT oven to 350°F.

For Crust
COMBINE graham cracker crumbs, butter and sugar in medium bowl; press onto bottom of ungreased 13×9-inch baking pan.

For Topping
MICROWAVE 1 cup morsels, sweetened condensed milk and vanilla extract in medium, uncovered, microwave-safe bowl on HIGH (100%) power for 1 minute. Stir. Morsels may retain some of their original shape. If necessary, microwave at additional 10- to 15-second intervals, stirring until morsels are melted. Pour evenly over crust. Top with nuts and remaining morsels.

BAKE for 20 to 25 minutes or until edges are bubbly. Cool completely in pan on wire rack. Cut into bars.

Makes 2 dozen bars

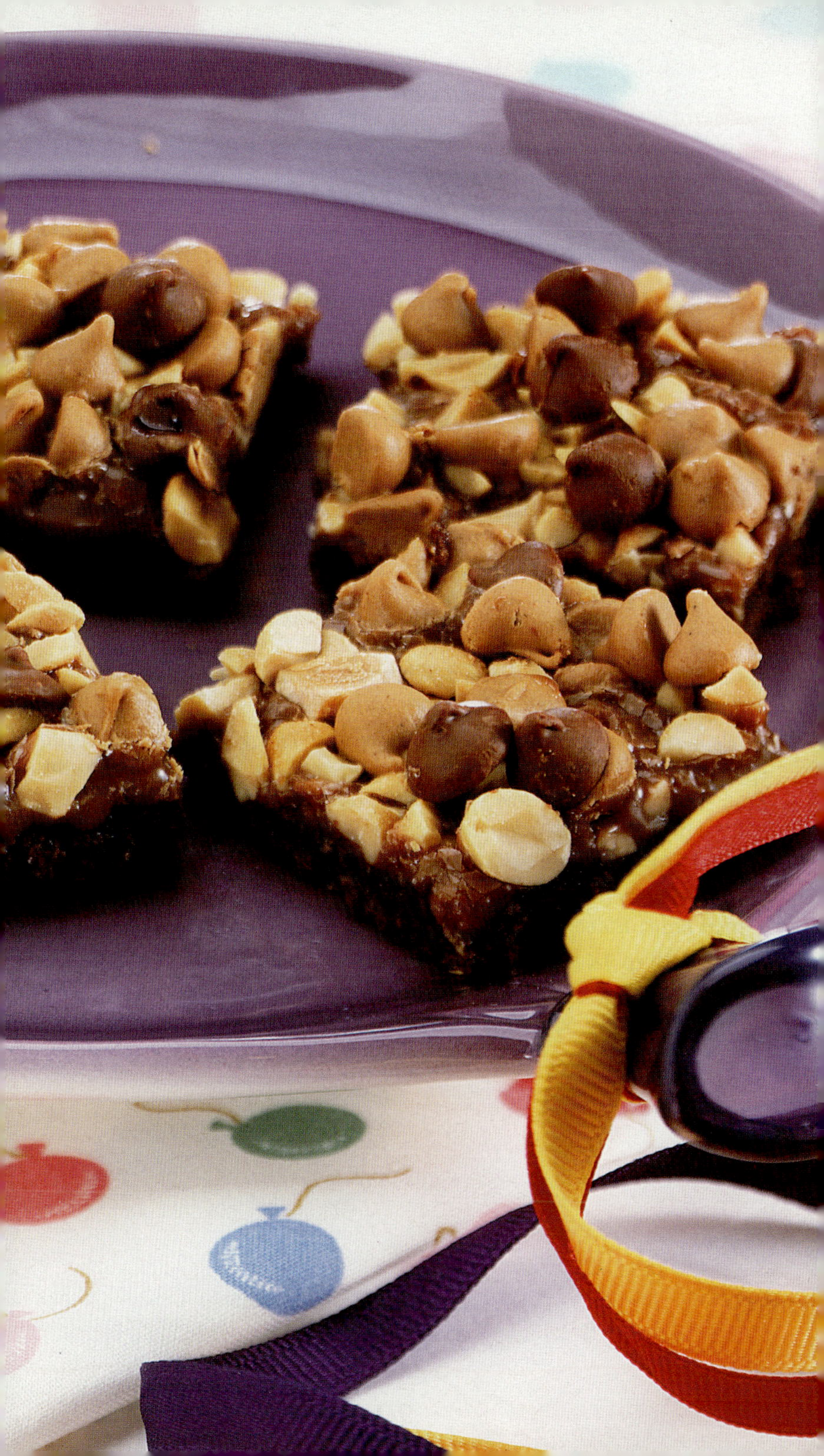

Pfeffernüsse

3½ cups all-purpose flour
2 teaspoons baking powder
1½ teaspoons ground cinnamon
1 teaspoon ground ginger
½ teaspoon baking soda
½ teaspoon salt
½ teaspoon ground cardamom
½ teaspoon ground cloves
¼ teaspoon black pepper
1 cup granulated sugar
1 cup butter, softened
¼ cup dark molasses
1 egg
Powdered sugar

1. Combine flour, baking powder, cinnamon, ginger, baking soda, salt, cardamom, cloves and pepper in large bowl.

2. Beat sugar and butter in large bowl with electric mixer at medium speed until light and fluffy. Beat in molasses and egg. Gradually add flour mixture. Beat at low speed until dough forms. Shape dough into disc; wrap in plastic wrap and refrigerate until firm, 30 minutes or up to 3 days.

3. Preheat oven to 350°F. Grease cookie sheets. Roll dough into 1-inch balls. Place 2 inches apart on prepared cookie sheets.

4. Bake 12 to 14 minutes or until golden brown. Transfer cookies to wire racks; dust with sifted powdered sugar. Cool completely. Store tightly covered at room temperature or freeze up to 3 months.

Makes about 5 dozen cookies

Cookies & Brownies

Spiced Raisin Cookies with White Chocolate Drizzle

2 cups all-purpose flour
1 teaspoon baking soda
1½ teaspoons ground cinnamon
1 teaspoon ground ginger
½ teaspoon ground allspice
¼ teaspoon salt
¾ cup butter, softened
1 cup sugar
¼ cup molasses
1 egg
1 cup SUN-MAID® Raisins or Golden Raisins
4 ounces white chocolate, coarsely chopped

HEAT oven to 375°F.

COMBINE flour, baking soda, cinnamon, ginger, allspice and salt in a small bowl. Set aside.

BEAT butter and sugar until light and fluffy.

ADD molasses and egg; beat well.

BEAT in raisins. Gradually beat in flour mixture on low speed just until incorporated.

DROP dough by tablespoonfuls onto ungreased cookie sheets 2 inches apart. Flatten dough slightly.

BAKE 12 to 14 minutes or until set. Cool on cookie sheets 1 minute; transfer to wire rack and cool completely.

MICROWAVE chocolate in a heavy, resealable plastic bag at high power 30 seconds. Turn bag over; heat additional 30 to 45 seconds or until almost melted. Knead bag with hands to melt remaining chocolate. Cut a ⅛-inch corner off one end of bag. Drizzle cooled cookies with chocolate. Let stand until chocolate is set, about 20 minutes.

Makes about 2 dozen cookies

Prep Time: 15 minutes
Baking Time: 14 minutes

Cookies & Brownies

Hershey's Soft & Chewy Cookies

1 cup (2 sticks) butter (no substitutes)
3/4 cup packed light brown sugar
1/2 cup granulated sugar
1/4 cup light corn syrup
1 egg
2 teaspoons vanilla extract
2 1/2 cups all-purpose flour
1 teaspoon baking soda
1/4 teaspoon salt
1 package (10 to 12 ounces) HERSHEY®'S Chips or Baking Bits (any flavor)

1. Heat oven to 350°F.

2. Beat butter, brown sugar and granulated sugar in large bowl until fluffy. Add corn syrup, egg and vanilla; beat well. Stir together flour, baking soda and salt; gradually add to butter mixture, beating until well blended. Stir in chips or bits. Drop by rounded teaspoons onto ungreased cookie sheet.

3. Bake 8 to 10 minutes or until lightly browned and almost set. Cool slightly; remove from cookie sheet to wire rack. Cool completely. Cookies will be softer the second day.

Makes about 3 1/2 dozen cookies

Chocolate Chocolate Cookies: *Decrease flour to 2 1/4 cups and add 1/4 cup HERSHEY®'S Cocoa or HERSHEY®'S Dutch Processed Cocoa.*

Hershey's Soft & Chewy Cookies

Acknowledgments

The publisher would like to thank the companies and organizations listed below for the use of their recipes and photographs in this publication.

Bob Evans®

Colorado Potato Administrative Committee

Del Monte Corporation

Dole Food Company, Inc.

Duncan Hines® and Moist Deluxe® are registered trademarks of Pinnacle Foods Corp.

EAGLE BRAND®

Grandma's® is a registered trademark of Mott's, LLP

The Hershey Company

Hillshire Farm®

Hormel Foods, LLC

Mrs. Dash®

National Honey Board

National Pork Board

Nestlé USA

New York Apple Association, Inc.

Northwest Cherry Growers

Reckitt Benckiser Inc.

Sargento® Foods Inc.

Sun•Maid® Growers of California

Reprinted with permission of Sunkist Growers, Inc. All Rights Reserved.

Unilever

Veg•All®

Index

A
Ambrosia, 77
Apple-Scotch Snack Cake, 64

B
Bacon and Maple Grits Puff, 46
Baked Apples, 71
Baked Apple Slices with Peanut Butter Crumble, 74
Banana Pudding, 70
Beef
   Beef Stroganoff Casserole, 24
   Cheeseburger Soup, 40
   Oven-Baked Stew, 26
Beef Stroganoff Casserole, 24
Berry Cobbler, 76
Buttermilk Oven-Fried Chicken, 4

C
Cakes
   Apple-Scotch Snack Cake, 64
   Hershey®s Red Velvet Cake, 60
   Orange Glazed Pound Cake, 58
   Pumpkin Carrot Cake, 62
   Sour Cream Cherry Cake, 65
Cheddar Broccoli Soup, 30
Cheeseburger Soup, 40
Cheesy Ham and Macaroni, 9
Chicken
   Buttermilk Oven-Fried Chicken, 4
   Chicken, Asparagus & Mushroom Bake, 22
   Chicken Rice Casserole, 21
   Country Chicken Chowder, 32
   Country Chicken Stew with Dumplings, 10
   Easy Chicken Salad, 38
   Family-Style Creamy Chicken and Noodles, 12
   Herbed Chicken & Vegetables, 2
   Homestyle Skillet Chicken, 14
Chicken, Asparagus & Mushroom Bake, 22
Chicken Rice Casserole, 21
Chilled Cherry Cheesecake, 66
Chocolate Chocolate Cookies, 92
Chocolate Peanut Butter Shortbread Bars, 82
Chunky Applesauce, 48
Cinnamon Toffee Sauce, 68
Classic Macaroni and Cheese, 20
Classic Rice Pudding, 77
Coconut Cream Pie, 58
Cookies
   Chocolate Peanut Butter Shortbread Bars, 82
   Dad's Ginger Molasses Cookies, 85
   Hershey®s Soft & Chewy Cookies, 92
   Layered Cookie Bars, 78
   Luscious Fresh Lemon Bars, 84
   Peanutty Gooey Bars, 88
   Pfeffernüsse, 90
   Pumpkin Spiced and Iced Cookies, 80
   Spiced Raisin Cookies with White Chocolate Drizzle, 91
Corn and Tomato Chowder, 42
Country Bean Soup, 34
Country Chicken Chowder, 32
Country Chicken Stew with Dumplings, 10
Country Green Beans with Turkey-Ham, 54
Cream Cheese Frosting, 62

D
Dad's Ginger Molasses Cookies, 85

E
Easy Chicken Salad, 38

F
Family-Style Creamy Chicken and Noodles, 12
Festive Cranberry Mold, 48

G
German Potato Salad, 37
Golden Corn Pudding, 50

Index

H
Ham
- Cheesy Ham and Macaroni, 9
- Chicken Rice Casserole, 21
- Country Green Beans with Turkey-Ham, 54
- Ham Loaf, 8
- Ham Pot Pie, 28
- Parsley, Ham and Pasta Salad, 40
- Ham Loaf, 8
- Ham Pot Pie, 28

Herbed Chicken & Vegetables, 2
Hershey₅s Red Velvet Cake, 60
Hershey₅s Soft & Chewy Cookies, 92
Homestyle Skillet Chicken, 14
Honeyed Beets, 54

I
Inside-Out Egg Salad, 37

K
Kentucky Cornbread & Sausage Stuffing, 51
Kielbasa & Sauerkraut Skillet Dinner, 6

L
Layered Cookie Bars, 78
Lemon Cheesecake, 72
Lemon Dream Pie, 56
Lit'l Smokies 'n' Macaroni 'n' Cheese, 28
Luscious Fresh Lemon Bars, 84

M
Maple-Mustard Pork Chops, 6

O
Orange Glazed Pound Cake, 58
Oven-Baked Stew, 26

P
Parsley, Ham and Pasta Salad, 40
Parsley Dumplings, 10
Peanutty Gooey Bars, 88

Pfeffernüsse, 90

Pork (*see also* **Ham; Sausage**)
- Ham Loaf, 8
- Maple-Mustard Pork Chops, 6
- Pork and Cabbage Soup, 36
- Pork with Savory Apple Stuffing, 16

Pork and Cabbage Soup, 36
Pork with Savory Apple Stuffing, 16
Potato Sausage Casserole, 18

Pumpkin
- Pumpkin Carrot Cake, 62
- Pumpkin Spiced and Iced Cookies, 80

R
Rocky Road Brownies, 86

S
Sausage
- Kentucky Cornbread & Sausage Stuffing, 51
- Kielbasa & Sauerkraut Skillet Dinner, 6
- Lit'l Smokies 'n' Macaroni 'n' Cheese, 28
- Potato Sausage Casserole, 18

Savory Skillet Broccoli, 44
Sour Cream Cherry Cake, 65
Spiced Raisin Cookies with White Chocolate Drizzle, 91
Sweet Potato Apple Bake, 51
Swiss-Style Vegetables, 52

T
Toffee Bread Pudding with Cinnamon Toffee Sauce, 68

V
Veg•All® Italian Soup, 38

W
Winter Fruit Compote, 71